Heinemann Plays

Night Must Fall

Heinemann Plays

Night Must Fall

A Play in Three Acts

Emlyn Williams

Heinemann

Heinemann Educational Bookd Ltd
Halley Court, Jordan Hill, Oxford OX2 8EJ
OXFORD LONDON EDINBURGH MADRID
ATHENS BOLOGNA MELBOURNE SYDNEY AUCKLAND
IBADAN NAIROBI GABORONE HARARE
KINGSTON PORTSMOUTH (NH) SINGAPORE

ISBN 0 435 20967 1

First published 1935
First published in the Drama Library 1961
Reprinted 1963, 1965, 1967, 1968, 1970,
1973, 1975, 1977, 1979

First published in the *Heinemann Plays* 1982
Reprinted 1984, 1986, 1988, 1990

Printed and bound in Great Britain by
Athenaeum Press Ltd., Newcastle upon Tyne.

CHARACTERS

THE LORD CHIEF JUSTICE
MRS BRAMSON
OLIVIA GRAYNE
HUBERT LAURIE
NURSE LIBBY
MRS TERENCE
DORA PARKOE
INSPECTOR BELSIZE
DAN

PROLOGUE
The Court of Criminal Appeal

The action of the play takes place in the sitting-room of 'Forest Corner', Mrs Bramson's bungalow in Essex

ACT ONE
A fine morning in October

ACT TWO
Scene 1: An afternoon, twelve days later
Scene 2: Late afternoon, two days later

ACT THREE
Scene 1: Half an hour later
Scene 2: Half an hour later

NIGHT MUST FALL *was first produced in London by J. P. Mitchelhill at the Duchess Theatre, on 31 May 1935 with the following cast:*

THE LORD CHIEF JUSTICE	Eric Stanley
MRS BRAMSON	May Whitty
OLIVIA GRAYNE	Angela Baddeley
HUBERT LAURIE	Basil Radford
NURSE LIBBY	Dorothy Langley
MRS TERENCE	Kathleen Harrison
DORA PARKOE	Betty Jardine
INSPECTOR BELSIZE	Matthew Boulton
DAN	Emlyn Williams

The play directed by
MILES MALLESON

BEFORE THE PLAY

*The orchestra plays light tunes until the house lights are turned
down; the curtain rises in darkness, accompanied by solemn
music: the opening chords of Holst's 'The Perfect Fool'.
A small light grows in the middle of the stage and shows
the* LORD CHIEF JUSTICE *sitting in judgment wearing
wig and red robes of office, in the Court of Criminal
Appeal. His voice, cold and disapproving, gradually swells
up with the light as he reaches his peroration.*

LORD CHIEF JUSTICE: . . . and there is no need to re-
capitulate here the arguments for and against this point
of law, which we heard in the long and extremely fair
summing up at the trial of the appellant at the Central
Criminal Court. The case was clearly put to the jury; and
it is against sentence of death for these two murders that
the prisoner now appeals. Which means that the last
stage of this important and extremely horrible case has
now been reached. On a later page in the summing up,
the learned judge, said this . . . (*Turning over papers*)
. . . 'This case has, through the demeanour of the prisoner
in the witness-box, obtained the most widespread and
scandalous publicity, which I would beg you most
earnestly, members of the jury, to forget.' I cannot help
but think that the deplorable atmosphere of sentimental
melodrama which has pervaded this trial has made the
theatre a more fitting background for it than a court of
law; but we are in a court of law, nevertheless, and the
facts have been placed before the court. A remarkable

and in my opinion praiseworthy feature of the case has been that the *sanity* of the prisoner has never been called into question; and, like the learned judge, the Court must dismiss as mischievous pretence the attitude of this young man who stands convicted of two brutal murders in cold blood. This case has, from beginning to end, exhibited no feature calling for sympathy; the evidence has on every point been conclusive, and on this evidence the jury have convicted the appellant. In the opinion of the Court there is no reason to interfere with that conviction, and this appeal must be dismissed.

The chords of solemn music are heard again, and the stage gradually darkens. A few seconds later the music merges into the sound of church bells playing far away, and the lights come up on

6

ACT I

*The sitting-room of Forest Corner, Mrs Bramson's bungalow in
a forest in Essex. A fine morning in October.*

*Centre back, a small hall; in its left side the front door
of the house (throughout the play, 'left' and 'right' refer to
the audience's left and right). Thick plush curtains can be
drawn across the entrance to the hall; they are open at the
moment. Windows, one on each side of the hall, with
window-seats and net curtains beyond which can be glimpsed
the pine-trees of the forest. In the left wall, upstage, a door
leading to the kitchen. In the left wall, downstage, the fireplace; above it, a cretonne-covered sofa, next to a very solid
cupboard built into the wall; below it a cane arm-chair. In
the right wall, upstage, a door leading to MRS BRAMSON'S
bedroom. In the right wall downstage, wide-open paned
doors leading to the sun-room. Right downstage, next the
sun-room, a large dining-table with four straight chairs
round it. Between the bedroom and the sun-room, a desk
with books on it, a cupboard below it, and a hanging mirror
on the wall above. Above the bedroom, a corner medicine
cupboard. Between the hall and the right window, an
occasional table.*

*The bungalow is tawdry but cheerful; it is built entirely
of wood, with an oil lamp fixed in the wall over the
occasional table. The room is comfortably furnished, though
in fussy and eccentric Victorian taste: stuffed birds, High-
land cattle in oils, antimacassars, and wax fruit are unobtrusively in evidence. On the mantelpiece, an ornate chiming
clock. The remains of breakfast on a tray on the table.*

MRS BRAMSON *is sitting in a wheeled chair in the centre*

of the room. She is a fussy, discontented, common woman of fifty-five, old-fashioned both in clothes and coiffure; NURSE LIBBY, *a kindly, matter-of-fact young north-country woman in district nurse's uniform, is sitting on the sofa, massaging one of her hands.* OLIVIA GRAYNE *sits on* MRS BRAMSON'S *right, holding a book; she is a subdued young woman of twenty-eight, her hair tied severely in a knot, wearing horn-rimmed spectacles; there is nothing in any way remarkable about her at the moment.* HUBERT LAURIE *is sitting in the arm-chair, scanning the 'Daily Telegraph'. He is thirty-five, moustached, hearty and pompous, wearing plus fours and smoking a pipe.*

A pause. The church bells die away.

MRS BRAMSON (*sharply*): Go on.

OLIVIA (*reading*): '. . . Lady Isabel humbly crossed her attenuated hands upon her chest. "I am on my way to God," she whispered, "to answer for all my sins and sorrows." "Child," said Miss Carlyle, "had I anything to do with sending you from . . . (*turning over*) . . . East Lynne?" Lady Isabel shook her head and cast down her gaze.'

MRS BRAMSON (*aggressively*): Now that's what I call a beautiful character.

NURSE: Very pretty. But the poor thing'd have felt that much better tucked up in 'ospital instead of lying about her own home, gassing her 'ead off——

MRS BRAMSON: Sh!

NURSE: Sorry.

OLIVIA (*reading*): ' "Thank God," inwardly breathed Miss Corny. . . . "Forgive me," she said loudly and in agitation. "I want to see Archibald," whispered Lady Isabel.'

Mrs Bramson: You don't see many books like *East Lynne* about nowadays.

Hubert: No, you don't.

Olivia (*reading*): ' "I want to see Archibald," whispered Lady Isabel. "I have prayed Joyce to bring him to me, and she will not——" '

Mrs Bramson (*sharply*): Olivia!

Olivia: Yes, auntie?

Mrs Bramson (*craftily*): You're not skipping, are you?

Olivia: Am I?

Mrs Bramson: You've missed out about Lady Isabel taking up her cross and the weight of it killing her. I may be a fool, but I do know *East Lynne*.

Olivia: Perhaps there were two pages stuck together.

Mrs Bramson: Very convenient when you want your walk, eh? Yes, I *am* a fool, I suppose, as well as an invalid.

Olivia: But I thought you were so much better——

Nurse: You'd two helpings of bacon at breakfast, remember——

Mrs Bramson: Doctor's orders. You know every mouthful's agony to me.

Hubert (*deep in his paper*): There's a man here in Weston-super-Mare who stood on his head for twenty minutes for a bet and he hasn't come to yet.

Mrs Bramson (*sharply*): I thought this morning I'd never be able to face the day.

Hubert: But last night when you opened the port——

Mrs Bramson: I've had a relapse since then. My heart's going like anything. Give me a chocolate.

> Olivia *rises and fetches her a chocolate from a large box on the table.*

Nurse: How does it feel?

MRS BRAMSON: Nasty. (*Munching her chocolate.*) I *know* it's neuritis.

NURSE: You know, Mrs Bramson, what you want isn't massage at all, only exercise. Your body——

MRS BRAMSON: Don't you dictate to me about my body. Nobody here understands my body or anything else about me. As for sympathy, I've forgotten the meaning of the word. (*To* OLIVIA.) What's the matter with your face?

OLIVIA (*startled*): I – I really don't know.

MRS BRAMSON: It's as long as my arm.

OLIVIA (*dryly*): I'm afraid it's made like that. (*She crosses the room, and comes back again.*)

MRS BRAMSON: What are you walking up and down for? What's the matter with you? Aren't you happy here?

OLIVIA: It's a bit lonely, but I'll get used to it.

MRS BRAMSON: Lonely? All these lovely woods? What *are* you talking about? Don't you like nature?

NURSE: Will that be all for today?

MRS BRAMSON: I suppose it'll have to be.

NURSE (*rising and taking her bag from the sofa*): Well, I've that confined lady still waiting in Shepperley. (*Going into the hall.*) Toodle-oo!

MRS BRAMSON: Mind you call Wednesday. In case my neuritis sets in again.

NURSE (*turning in the hall*): I will that. And if paralysis pops up, let me know. Toodle-oo!

> *She marches cheerily out of the front door.* MRS BRAM-
> SON *cannot make up her mind if the last remark is sarcastic
> or not. She concentrates on* OLIVIA.

MRS BRAMSON: You know, you mustn't think just because this house is lonely you're going to get a rise in salary. Oh no . . . I expect you've an idea I'm worth a good bit of money, haven't you? . . . It isn't my money you're after, is it?

OLIVIA (*setting chairs to rights round the table*): I'm sorry, but my sense of humour can't stand the strain. I'll have to go.

MRS BRAMSON: Can you afford to go?

OLIVIA (*after a pause, controlling herself*): You know I can't.

MRS BRAMSON: Then don't talk such nonsense. Clear the breakfast things.

OLIVIA *hesitates, then crosses to the kitchen door*.

(*Muttering*.) Sense of humour indeed, never heard of such a thing.

OLIVIA (*at the door*): Mrs Terence, will you clear away? (*She goes to the left window, and looks out.*)

MRS BRAMSON: You wait, my girl. Pride comes before a fall. Won't catch a husband with your nose in the air, you know.

OLIVIA: I don't want a husband.

MRS BRAMSON: Don't like men, I suppose? Never heard of them, I suppose? Don't believe you. See?

OLIVIA (*resigned*): I see. It's going to be a fine day.

MRS BRAMSON (*taking up 'East Lynne' from the table*): It'll cloud over, I expect.

OLIVIA: I don't think so. The trees look beautiful with the sun on them. Everything looks so clean. (*Lifting up three books from the window-seat.*) Shall I pack the other half of Mrs Henry Wood?

MRS BRAMSON: Mrs Henry Wood? Who's Mrs Henry Wood? Pack the other half of Mrs Henry Wood? What *are* you talking about?

OLIVIA: She wrote your favourite book – *East Lynne*.

MRS BRAMSON (*looking at her book*): Oh . . . (*Picking a paper out of it.*) What's this? (*Reading ponderously.*) A sonnet. 'The flame of passion is not red but white, not quick but slow——'

OLIVIA (*going to her and snatching it from her with a cry*): Don't!

MRS BRAMSON: Writing *poetry*! That's a hobby and a half, I must say! 'Flame of passion . . .' *Well!*

OLIVIA (*crossing to the fireplace*): It's only a silly poem I amused myself with at college. It's not meant for anybody but me.

MRS BRAMSON: You're a dark horse, you are.

> MRS TERENCE *enters from the kitchen. She is the cook, middle-aged, Cockney and fearless. She carries a bunch of roses.*

MRS TERENCE (*grimly*): Would you be wanting anything?

MRS BRAMSON: Yes. Clear away.

MRS TERENCE: That's Dora's job. Where's Dora?

OLIVIA: She's gone into the clearing for some firewood.

MRS BRAMSON: You can't expect the girl to gather firewood with one hand and clear breakfast with the other. Clear away.

MRS TERENCE (*crossing to the table, under her breath*): All right, you sour-faced old hag.

> HUBERT *drops his pipe.* MRS BRAMSON *winces and looks away.* MRS TERENCE *clears the table.*

HUBERT (*to* OLIVIA): What – what was that she said?

MRS TERENCE: She 'eard. And then she 'as to save 'er face and pretend she 'asn't. She knows nobody but me'd stay with 'er a day if I went.

Mrs Bramson: She oughtn't to talk to me like that. I know she steals my sugar.

Mrs Terence: That's a living lie. (*Going round to her.*) Here are your roses.

Mrs Bramson: You've cut them too young. I knew you would.

Mrs Terence (*taking up her tray and starting for the kitchen*): Then you come out and pick the ones you want, and you'll only 'ave yourself to blame.

Mrs Bramson: That's a nice way to talk to an invalid.

Mrs Terence: If you're an invalid, I'm the Prince of Wales. (*She goes back into the kitchen.*)

Olivia: Would you like me to read some more?

Mrs Bramson: No. I'm upset for the day now. I'd better see she does pick the right roses. (*Wheeling herself, muttering.*) That woman's a menace. Good mind to bring an action against her. She ought to be put away. . . . (*Shouting.*) Wait for me, wait for me!

> Her voice dies away in the kitchen. The kitchen door closes. Hubert *and* Olivia *are alone.*

Olivia: That's the fifth action she threatened to bring this week. (*She crosses to the right window.*)

Hubert: She's a good one to talk about putting away. Crikey! She'll be found murdered one of these days. . . . (*Suddenly reading from his paper.*) 'In India a population of three and a half hundred million is loyal to Britain; now——'

Olivia: Oh, Hubert! (*Good-humouredly.*) I thought I'd cured you of that.

Hubert: Sorry.

Olivia: You've only had two weeks of her. I've had six. (*A pause. She sighs restlessly.*)

HUBERT: Fed up?

OLIVIA: It's such a very inadequate expression, don't you think; . . . (*After a pause.*) How bright the sun is today. . . . (*She is pensive, far-away, smiling.*)

HUBERT: A penny for 'em.

OLIVIA: I was just thinking . . . I often wonder on a very fine morning what it'll be like . . . for night to come. And I never can. And yet it's got to. . . . (*Looking at his perplexed face.*) It *is* silly, isn't it?

> DORA *comes in from the kitchen with a duster and crosses towards the bedroom. She is a pretty, stupid, and rather sluttish country girl of twenty, wearing a maid's uniform. She looks depressed.*

Who are those men, Dora?

DORA: What men, miss?

OLIVIA: Over there, behind the clearing.

DORA: Oh. . . . (*Peering past her.*) Oh. 'Adn't seen them. What are they doing poking about in that bush?

OLIVIA (*absently*): I don't know. I saw them yesterday, too, further down the woods.

DORA (*lamely*): I expect they're looking for something. (*She goes into the kitchen.*)

HUBERT: She looks a bit off-colour, doesn't she?

OLIVIA: The atmosphere must be getting her down, too.

HUBERT: I'm wondering if I'm going to be able to stand it myself. Coming over here every day for another week.

OLIVIA (*smiling*): There's nothing to prevent you staying at *home* every day for another week . . . is there?

HUBERT (*still apparently reading the paper*): Oh yes, there is. What d'you think I invite myself to lunch every day for? You don't think it's the old geyser, do you?

OLIVIA (*smiling*): No. (*She comes down to the table.*)

HUBERT: Don't want to sound rude, et cetera, but women don't get men proposing to them every day, you know. . . . (*Turning over a page.*) Gosh, what a wizard machine——

OLIVIA (*sitting at the left of the table*): I can't think *why* you want to marry me, as a matter of fact. It isn't the same as if I were very pretty, or something.

HUBERT: You do say some jolly rum things, Olivia, upon my soul.

OLIVIA: I'll tell *you* why, then, if it makes you feel any better. You're cautious; and you want to marry me because I'm quiet. I'd make you a steady wife, and run a home for you

HUBERT: There's nothing to be ashamed of in being steady. I'm steady myself.

OLIVIA: I know you are.

HUBERT: Then why aren't you keen?

OLIVIA (*after a pause, tolerant but weary*): Because you're an unmitigated bore.

HUBERT: A bore? (*Horrified.*) *Me*, a bore? Upon my word, Olivia, I think you're a bit eccentric, I do really. Sorry to be rude, and all that, but that's put the kybosh on it! People could call me a thing or two, but I've never been called a bore!

OLIVIA: Bores never are. People are too bored with them to call them anything.

HUBERT: I suppose you'd be more likely to say 'Yes' if I were an unmitigated bounder?

OLIVIA (*with a laugh*): Oh, don't be silly. . . .

HUBERT (*going to her*): You're a rum girl, Olivia, upon my soul you are. P'raps that's why I think you're so jolly attractive. Like a mouse one minute, and then this straight-from-the-shoulder business. . . . What *is* a sonnet?

OLIVIA: It's a poem of fourteen lines.

HUBERT: Oh yes, Shakespeare. . . . Never knew you did a spot of rhyming, Olivia! Now that's what I mean about you. . . . We'll have to start calling you Elizabeth Brontë! (*She turns away. He studies her.*) You *are* bored, aren't you?

　　　He walks to the sun-room. She rouses herself and turns
　　　to him impetuously.

OLIVIA: I'm being silly, I know – of course I *ought* to get married, and *of course* this is a wonderful chance, and——

HUBERT (*moving to her*): Good egg! Then you will?

OLIVIA (*stalling*): Give me a – another week or two – will you?

HUBERT: Oh. My holiday's up on the twenty-seventh.

OLIVIA: I know I'm being tiresome, but——

MRS BRAMSON (*in the kitchen*): The most disgraceful thing I've ever heard——

HUBERT: She's coming back. . . .

　　　OLIVIA *rises and goes to the right window.* HUBERT *hur-*
　　　ries into the sun-room. MRS BRAMSON *is wheeled back from*
　　　the kitchen by MRS TERENCE, *to the centre of the room.*
　　　She (MRS BRAMSON) *has found the pretext for the scene*
　　　she has been longing to make since she got up this morning.

MRS BRAMSON: Fetch that girl here. This minute.

MRS TERENCE: Oh, leave the child alone.

MRS BRAMSON: Leave her alone, the little sneak-thief? Fetch her here.

MRS TERENCE (*at the top of her voice*): Dora! (*Opening the front door and calling into the trees.*) Dora!

OLIVIA: What's Dora done now?

MRS BRAMSON: Broken three of my Crown Derby,

that's all. Thought if she planted them in the rose-bed I wouldn't be well enough to see them, I suppose. Well, I *have* seen.

MRS TERENCE (*crossing and calling to the bedroom*): You're wanted.

DORA'S VOICE: What for?

MRS TERENCE: She wants to kiss you good morning, what d'you think. . . .

> *She collects the table cloth, fetches a vase from the mantelpiece, and goes into the kitchen.* DORA *enters gingerly from the bedroom carrying a cup and saucer on a tray.*

DORA: Did you want me, mum?

MRS BRAMSON: Crown Derby to you, my girl.

DORA (*uncertain*): Beg pardon, mum?

MRS BRAMSON: I suppose you think that china came from Marks and Spencer?

DORA: Oh . . . (*Snivelling.*) Oh . . . oh . . .

OLIVIA (*coming between* DORA *and* MRS BRAMSON): Come along, Dora, it's not as bad as all that.

DORA: Oh yes, it is. . . . Oh . . .

MRS BRAMSON: You can leave, that's all. You can leave.

> *Appalled,* DORA *drops the tray and breaks the saucer.*

That settles it. Now you'll *have* to leave.

DORA (*with a cry*): Oh, please I . . . (*Kneeling and collecting broken china.*) Oh, ma'am – I'm not meself, you see. . . . (*Snivelling.*) I'm in – terrible trouble. . . .

MRS BRAMSON: Have you been stealing?

DORA (*shocked*): Oh no!

OLIVIA (*after a pause*): Are you going to have a baby?

> *After a pause,* DORA *nods.*

DORA (*putting the china in her apron*): The idea of me stealing . . . I do go to Sunday School anyways. . . .

MRS BRAMSON: So that's the game. Wouldn't think

butter would melt in her mouth. . . . You'll have to go, of course; I can't have that sort of thing in this house – and stop squeaking! You'll bring my heart on again. It's all this modern life. I've always said so. All these films and rubbish.

OLIVIA: My dear auntie, you can't have a baby by just sitting in the pictures.

MRS BRAMSON: Go away, and don't interefere.

OLIVIA *goes to the left window*. DORA *rises*.

(*Triumphantly*.) So you're going to have a child. When?

DORA (*sniffling*): Last August Bank Holiday. . . .

MRS BRAMSON: What? . . . Oh!

DORA: I 'aven't got a penny only what I earn – and if I lose my job 'ere——

MRS BRAMSON: He'll have to marry you.

DORA: Oh, I don't think he's keen. . . .

MRS BRAMSON: I'll *make* him keen. Who is the gentleman?

DORA: A boy I know; Dan his name is – leas' 'e's not a gentleman. He's a page-boy at the Tallboys.

MRS BRAMSON: The Tallboys? D'you mean that new-fangled place all awnings and loud-speakers and things?

DORA: That's right. On the by-pass.

MRS BRAMSON: Just the nice ripe sort of place for mischief, it always looked to me. All those lanterns. . . What's his character, the good-for-nothing scoundrel?

DORA: Oh, he's nice, really. He done the wrong thing by me, but he's all right, if you know what I mean. . .

MRS BRAMSON: No, I don't. Where does he come from?

DORA: He's sort of Welsh, I think. 'E's been to sea, too. He's funny of course. Ever so open. Baby-face, they call him. Though I never seem to get 'old of what 'e's thinking somehow——

MRS BRAMSON: I'll get hold of what he's thinking, all right. I've had my knife into that sort ever since I was a girl.

DORA: Oh, mum, if I got him to let you speak to him – d'you think, I could stay on?

MRS BRAMSON (*after a pause*): If he marries you at once.

DORA: Shall I—— (*Eagerly.*) As a matter of fact, ma'am, he's gone on a message on his bicycle to Payley Hill this morning, and he said he might pop in to see me on the way back——

MRS BRAMSON: That's right; nothing like visitors to brighten your mornings, eh? I'll deal with him.

DORA: Yes. . . . (*Going, and turning at the kitchen door, in impulsive relief.*) Oh, ma'am——

MRS BRAMSON: And I'll stop the Crown Derby out of your wages.

DORA (*crestfallen*): Oh!

MRS BRAMSON: What were you going to say?

DORA: Well, ma'am, I *was* going to say I don't know how to thank you for your generosity. . . .

She goes into the kitchen. The clock chimes.

MRS BRAMSON: Olivia!

OLIVIA: Yes, auntie?

MRS BRAMSON: You've forgotten again. Medicine's overdue. Most important.

OLIVIA *crosses to the medicine cupboard and fetches the medicine. MRS TERENCE comes in from the kitchen with a vase of flowers and barges between the sofa and the wheel-chair.*

MRS TERENCE (*muttering*): All this furniture. . . .

MRS BRAMSON (*to her*): Did *you* know she's having a baby?

MRS TERENCE (*coldly*): She did mention it in conversation.

Mrs Bramson: Playing with fire, that's the game now-adays.

Mrs Terence (*arranging flowers as* Olivia *gives* Mrs Bramson *her medicine*): Playing with fiddlesticks. We're only young once; that 'ot summer too. She's been a fool, but she's no criminal. And, talking of criminals, there's a p'liceman at the kitchen door.

Mrs Bramson: A what?

Mrs Terence: A p'liceman. A bobby.

Mrs Bramson: What does he want?

Mrs Terence: Better ask 'im. I know *my* conscience is clear; I don't know about other people's.

Mrs Bramson: But I've never had a policeman coming to see me before!

Dora *runs in from the kitchen.*

Dora (*terrified*): There's a man there! From the p'lice! 'E said something about the Tallboys! 'E—'e 'asn't come about me, 'as 'e?

Mrs Terence: Of course, he 'asn't——

Mrs Bramson: He may have.

Mrs Terence: Don't frighten the girl; she's simple enough now.

Mrs Bramson (*sharply*): It's against the law, what she's done, isn't it? (*To* Dora.) Go back in there till he sends for you.

Dora *creeps back into the kitchen.*

Olivia (*at the left window*): He isn't a policeman, as a matter of fact. He must be a plain-clothes man.

Mrs Terence (*sardonically*): Scotland Yard, I should think.

Belsize *is seen outside, crossing the left window to the front door.*

MRS BRAMSON: That place in those detective books? Don't be so silly.

MRS TERENCE: He says he wants to see you very particular——

A sharp rat-tat at the front door.

(*Going to the hall.*) On a very particular matter. . . . (*Turning on* MRS BRAMSON.) And don't you start callin' me silly! (*Going to the front door, and opening it.*) This way, sir. . . .

> BELSIZE *enters, followed by* MRS TERENCE. *He is an entirely inconspicuous man of fifty, dressed in tweeds; his suavity hides an amount of strength.*

BELSIZE: Mrs Bramson? I'm sorry to break in on you like this. My card . . .

MRS BRAMSON (*taking it, sarcastically*): I suppose you're going to tell me you're from Scotland Ya—— (*She sees the name on the card.*)

BELSIZE: I see you've all your wits about you!

MRS BRAMSON: Oh. (*Reading incredulously.*) Criminal Investigation Department!

BELSIZE (*smiling*): A purely informal visit, I assure you.

MRS BRAMSON: I don't like having people in my house that I don't know.

BELSIZE (*the velvet glove*): I'm afraid the law sometimes makes it necessary.

> MRS TERENCE *gives him a chair next the table. He sits.*
> MRS TERENCE *stands behind the table.*

MRS BRAMSON (*to her*): You can go.

MRS TERENCE: I don't want to go. I might 'ave to be arrested for stealing sugar.

BELSIZE: Sugar? . . . As a matter of fact you might be useful. Any of you may be useful. Mind my pipe?

MRS BRAMSON *blows in disgust and waves her hand before her face.*

MRS BRAMSON: Is it about my maid having an illegitimate child?

BELSIZE: I beg your pardon? . . . Oh no! That sort of thing's hardly in my line, thank God. . . . Lonely spot. . . . (*To* MRS TERENCE.) Long way for you to walk every day, isn't it?

MRS TERENCE: I don't walk. I cycle.

BELSIZE: Oh.

MRS BRAMSON: What's the matter?

BELSIZE: I just thought if she walked she might use some of the paths, and have seen – something.

MRS BRAMSON: Something of what?

MRS TERENCE: Something?

BELSIZE: I'll tell you. I——

A piano is heard in the sun-room, playing the 'Merry Widow' waltz.

(*Casually*.) Other people in the house?

MRS BRAMSON (*calling sharply*): Mr Laurie!

The piano stops.

HUBERT'S VOICE (*as the piano stops in the sun-room*): Yes?

MRS BRAMSON (*to* OLIVIA *sourly*): Did *you* ask him to play the piano?

HUBERT *comes back from the sun-room.*

HUBERT (*breezily*): Hello, house on fire or something?

MRS BRAMSON: Very nearly. This is Mr-er-Bel——

BELSIZE: Belsize.

MRS BRAMSON (*dryly*): Of Scotland Yard.

HUBERT: Oh . . . (*Apprehensive.*) It isn't about my car, is it?

BELSIZE: No.

HUBERT: Oh. (*Shaking hands affably.*) How do you do?

22

BELSIZE: How do you do, sir . . .

MRS BRAMSON: He's a friend of Miss Grayne's here. Keeps calling.

BELSIZE: Been calling long?

MRS BRAMSON: Every day for two weeks. Just before lunch.

HUBERT: Well——

OLIVIA (*sitting on the sofa*): Perhaps I'd better introduce myself. I'm Olivia Grayne, Mrs Bramson's niece. I work for her.

BELSIZE: Oh, I see. Thanks. Well now . . .

HUBERT (*sitting at the table, effusively*): I know a chap on the Stock Exchange who was taken last year and shown over the Black Museum at Scotland Yard.

BELSIZE (*politely*): Really——

MRS BRAMSON: And what d'you expect the policeman to do about it?

HUBERT: Well, it was very interesting, he said. Bit ghoulish, of course——

BELSIZE: I expect so. . . . (*Getting down to business.*) Now I wonder if any of you've seen anything in the least out of the ordinary round here lately? Anybody called – anybody strange wandering about in the woods – overheard anything?

They look at one another.

MRS BRAMSON: The only visitor's been the doctor – and the district nurse.

MRS TERENCE: Been ever so gay.

HUBERT: As a matter of fact, funny thing did happen to me. Tuesday afternoon it was, I remember now.

BELSIZE: Oh?

HUBERT(*graphically*): I was walking back to my cottage

from golf, and I heard something moving stealthily behind a tree, or a bush, or something.

BELSIZE (*interested*): Oh, yes?

HUBERT: Turned out to be a squirrel.

MRS BRAMSON (*in disgust*): Oh! . . .

HUBERT: No bigger than my hand! Funny thing to happen, I thought.

BELSIZE: Very funny. Anything else?

HUBERT: Not a thing. By Jove, fancy walking in the woods and stumbling over a dead body! Most embarrassing!

MRS TERENCE: I've stumbled over bodies in them woods afore now. But they wasn't dead. Oh no.

MRS BRAMSON: Say what you know, and don't talk so much.

MRS TERENCE: Well, I've told 'im all I've seen. A bit o' love now and again. Though 'ow they make do with all them pine-needles beats me.

BELSIZE: Anything else?

MRS BRAMSON: Miss Grayne's always moping round the woods. Perhaps *she* can tell you something.

OLIVIA: I haven't seen anything, I'm afraid. . . . Oh – I saw some men beating the undergrowth——

BELSIZE: Yes, I'm coming to that. But no tramps, for instance.

OLIVIA: N-No. I don't think so.

HUBERT: Always carry a stick's my motto, I'd like to see a tramp try anything on with me. A-ha! Swish!

MRS BRAMSON: What's all the fuss about? Has there been a robbery, or something?

BELSIZE: There's a lady missing.

MRS TERENCE: Where from?

BELSIZE: The Tallboys.

MRS BRAMSON: That Tallboys again——

BELSIZE: A Mrs Chalfont.

MRS TERENCE: Chalfont? Oh yes! Dyed platinum blonde – widow of a colonel, so she says, livin' alone, so she says, always wearing them faldalaldy open-work stockings. Fond of a drop too. That's 'er.

HUBERT: Why, d'you know her?

MRS TERENCE: Never set eyes on 'er. But you know how people talk. Partial to that there, too, I'm told.

MRS BRAMSON: What's that there?

MRS TERENCE: Ask no questions, I'll tell no lies.

BELSIZE (*quickly*): Well, anyway . . . Mrs Chalfont left the Tallboys last Friday afternoon without a hat, went for a walk through the woods in this direction, and has never been seen since. (*He makes his effect.*)

MRS BRAMSON: I expect she was so drunk she fell flat and never came to.

BELSIZE: We've had the woods pretty well thrashed. (*To* OLIVIA.) Those would be the men you saw. Now she was . . .

HUBERT (*taking the floor*): She may have had a brain-storm, you know, and taken a train somewhere. That's not uncommon you know, among people of her sort. (*Airing knowledge.*) And if what we gather from our friend here's true – and she's both a dipsomaniac *and* a nympho-maniac——

MRS BRAMSON: Hark at the walking dictionary!

BELSIZE: We found her bag in her room; and maniacs can't get far without cash . . . however dipso or nympho they may be. . . .

HUBERT: Oh.

BELSIZE: She was a very flashy type of wo—she *is* a flashy type, I should say. At least I hope I should say. . . .

MRS BRAMSON: What d'you mean? Why d'you hope?

BELSIZE: Well . . .

OLIVIA: You don't mean she may be . . . she mayn't be alive?

BELSIZE: It's possible.

MRS BRAMSON: You'll be saying she's been murdered next!

BELSIZE: That's been known.

MRS BRAMSON: Lot of stuff and nonsense. From a policeman, too. Anybody'd think you'd been brought up on penny dreadfuls.

> OLIVIA *turns and goes to the window.*

BELSIZE (*to* MRS BRAMSON): Did you see about the fellow being hanged for the Ipswich murder? In last night's papers?

MRS BRAMSON: I've lived long enough not to believe the papers.

BELSIZE: They occasionally print facts. And murder's occasionally a fact.

HUBERT: Everybody likes a good murder, as the saying goes! Remember those trials in the *Evening Standard* last year! Jolly interesting. I followed——

BELSIZE (*rising*): I'd be very grateful if you'd all keep your eyes and ears open, just in case. . . . (*Shaking hands.*) Good morning . . . good morning . . . good morning, Mrs Bramson. I must apologise again for intruding——

> *He turns to* OLIVIA *who is still looking out of the window.*

Good morning, Miss . . . er . . .

> *A pause.*

OLIVIA (*starting*): I'm so sorry.

BELSIZE: Had you remembered something?

OLIVIA: Oh no . . .

26

MRS BRAMSON: What were you thinking, then?

OLIVIA: Only how . . . strange it is.

BELSIZE: What?

OLIVIA: Well, here we all are, perfectly ordinary English people. We woke up . . . no, it's silly.

MRS BRAMSON: Of course it's silly.

BELSIZE (*giving* MRS BRAMSON *an impatient look*): No, go on.

OLIVIA: Well, we woke up this morning, thinking, 'Here's another day.' We got up, looked at the weather, and talked; and here we all are, still talking. . . . And all that time——

MRS BRAMSON: My dear girl, who are you to expect a policeman——

BELSIZE (*quelling her sternly*): If you please! I want to hear what she's got to say. (*To* OLIVIA.) Well?

OLIVIA: All that time . . . there may be something . . . lying in the woods. Hidden under a bush, with two feet just showing. Perhaps one high heel catching the sunlight, with a bird perched on the end of it; and the other – a stockinged foot, with blood . . . that's dried into the openwork stocking. And there's a man walking about somewhere, and talking, like us; and he woke up this morning, and looked at the weather. . . . And he killed her. . . . (*Smiling, looking out of the window.*) The cat doesn't believe a word of it anyway. It's just walking away.

MRS BRAMSON: Well!

MRS TERENCE: Ooh, Miss Grayne, you give me the creeps! I'm glad it *is* morning, that's all I can say. . . .

BELSIZE: I don't think the lady can quite describe *herself* as ordinary, after that little flight of fancy!

MRS BRAMSON: Oh, that's nothing; she writes poetry. Jingle jingle——

BELSIZE: I can only hope she's wrong, or it'll mean a nice job of work for us! . . . Well, if anything funny happens, nip along to Shepperley police station. Pity you're not on the phone. Good morning. . . . Good morning.

MRS TERENCE: This way. . . . (*She follows* BELSIZE *into the hall.*)

BELSIZE: No, don't bother. . . . Good morning. . . .

He goes out. MRS TERENCE *shuts the door after him.*

MRS BRAMSON (*to* HUBERT): What are *you* staring at?

HUBERT (*crossing to the fireplace*): Funny, I can't get out of my mind what Olivia said about the man being somewhere who's done it.

MRS TERENCE (*coming into the room*): Why, Mr Laurie, it might be you! After all, there's nothing in your face that *proves* it isn't!

HUBERT: Oh, come, come! You're being a bit hard on the old countenance, aren't you?

MRS TERENCE: Well, 'e's not going to walk about with bloodshot eyes and a snarl all over his face, is he? (*She goes into the kitchen.*)

HUBERT: That's true enough.

MRS BRAMSON: Missing woman indeed! She's more likely than not at this very moment sitting in some saloon bar. On the films, I shouldn't wonder. (*To* OLIVIA.) Pass me my wool, will you . . .

OLIVIA *crosses to the desk. A knock at the kitchen door.* DORA *appears, cautiously.*

DORA: *Was* it about me?

OLIVIA: Of course it wasn't.

DORA (*relieved*): Oh . . . please, mum, 'e's 'ere.

MRS BRAMSON: Who?

DORA: My boy fr—my gentleman friend, ma'am, from the Tallboys.

MRS BRAMSON: I'm ready for him. (*Waving aside the wool which* OLIVIA *brings to her.*) The sooner he's made to realise what his duty is, the better. I'll give him baby-face!

DORA: Thank you, ma'am. (*She goes out through the front door.*)

HUBERT: What gentleman? What duty?

OLIVIA: The maid's going to have a baby. (*She crosses and puts the wool in the cupboard of the desk.*)

HUBERT: Is she, by Jove! . . . Don't look at me like that, Mrs Bramson! I've only been in the country two weeks. . . . But is *he* from the Tallboys?

MRS BRAMSON: A page-boy or something of the sort.

    DORA *comes back to the front door, looks back and beckons. She is followed by* DAN, *who saunters past her into the room. He is a young fellow wearing a blue pillbox hat, uniform trousers, a jacket too small for him, and bicycle-clips: the stub of a cigarette dangles between his lips. He speaks with a rough accent, indeterminate, but more Welsh than anything else.*

    His personality varies very considerably as the play proceeds: the impression he gives at the moment is one of totally disarming good humour and childlike unselfconsciousness. It would need a very close observer to suspect that there is something wrong somewhere – that this personality is completely assumed. DORA *shuts the front door and comes to the back of the sofa.*

MRS BRAMSON (*sternly*): Well?

DAN (*saluting*): Mornin', all!

MRS BRAMSON: So you're Baby-face?

DAN: That's me. (*Grinning*). Silly name, isn't it? (*After a pause.*) I must apologise to all and sundry for this fancy dress, but it's my working togs. I been on duty this mornin', and my hands isn't very clean. You see, I didn't know as it was going to be a party.

MRS BRAMSON: Party?

DAN (*looking at* OLIVIA): Well, it's ladies, isn't it?

HUBERT: Are you shy with ladies?

DAN (*smiling at* OLIVIA): Oh yes.

OLIVIA *moves away coldly.* DAN *turns to* MRS BRAMSON.

MRS BRAMSON (*cutting*): You smoke, I see.

DAN: Yes. (*Taking the stub out of his mouth with alacrity and taking off his hat.*) Oh, I'm sorry. I always forget my manners with a cigarette when I'm in company. . . . (*Pushing the stub behind his ear, as* OLIVIA *crosses to the armchair.*) I always been clumsy in people's houses. I am sorry.

MRS BRAMSON: You know my maid, Dora Parkoe, I believe?

DAN: Well, we have met, yes. . . . (*With a grin at* DORA.)

MRS BRAMSON (*to* DORA): Go away!

DORA *creeps back into the kitchen.*

You walked out with her last August Bank Holiday?

DAN: Yes. . . . Excuse me smiling, but it sounds funny when you put it like that, doesn't it?

MRS BRAMSON: You ought to be ashamed of yourself.

DAN (*soberly*): Oh, I am.

MRS BRAMSON: How did it happen?

DAN (*embarrassed*): Well . . . we went . . . did *you* have a nice Bank Holiday?

MRS BRAMSON: Answer my question!

HUBERT: Were you in love with the wench?

DAN: Oh yes!

30

MRS BRAMSON (*triumphantly*): *When* did you first meet her?

DAN: Er-Bank Holiday morning.

MRS BRAMSON: Picked her up, I suppose?

DAN: Oh no, I didn't pick her up! I asked her for a match, and then I took her for a bit of a walk, to take her mind off her work——

HUBERT: You seem to have succeeded.

DAN (*smiling at him, then catching* MRS BRAMSON'S *eye*): I've thought about it a good bit since, I can tell you. Though it's a bit awkward talking about it in front of strangers; though you all look very nice people; but it is a *bit* awkward——

HUBERT: I should jolly well think it is awkward for a chap! Though of course, never having been in the same jam myself——

MRS BRAMSON: I haven't finished with him yet.

HUBERT: In that case I'm going for my stroll. . . . (*He makes for the door to the hall.*)

OLIVIA: You work at the Tallboys, don't you?

DAN: Yes, miss. (*Grinning.*) Twenty-four hours a day, miss.

HUBERT (*coming to* DAN'S *left*): Then perhaps you can tell us something about the female who's been murdered.

> *An unaccountable pause.* DAN *looks slowly from* OLIVIA *to* HUBERT *and back again.*

Well, *can* you tell us? You know there was a Mrs Chalfont staying at the Tallboys who went off one day?

DAN: Yes.

HUBERT: And nobody's seen her since?

DAN: I know.

MRS BRAMSON: What's she like?

DAN (*to* MRS BRAMSON): But I thought you said – or somebody said – something about – a murder?

HUBERT: Oh, we don't *know*, of course, but there *might* have been, mightn't there?

DAN (*suddenly effusive*): Yes, there might have been, yes!

HUBERT: Ever seen her?

DAN: Oh, yes. I used to take cigarettes an' drinks for her.

MRS BRAMSON (*impatiently*): What's she *like*?

DAN: What's she like? . . . (*To* MRS BRAMSON.) She's . . . on the tall side. Thin ankles, with one o' them bracelets on one of 'em. (*Looking at* OLIVIA.) Fair hair—— (*A sudden thought seems to arrest him. He goes on looking at* OLIVIA.)

MRS BRAMSON: Well? Go on!

DAN (*after a pause, in a level voice*): Thin eyebrows, with white marks, where they was pulled out . . . to be in the fashion, you know. . . . Her mouth . . . a bit thin as well, with red stuff painted round it, to make it look more; you can rub it off . . . I suppose. Her neck . . . rather thick. Laughs a bit loud; and then it stops. (*After a pause.*) She's . . . very lively. (*With a quick smile that dispels the atmosphere he has unaccountably created.*) You can't say I don't keep my eyes skinned, can you?

HUBERT: I should say you do! A living portrait, if ever there was one, what? Now——

MRS BRAMSON (*pointedly*): Weren't you going for a walk?

HUBERT: So I was, by Jove! Well, I'll charge off. Bye-bye. (*He goes out of the front door.*)

OLIVIA (*her manner faintly hostile*): You're very observant.

DAN: Well, the ladies, you know . . .

32

Mrs Bramson: If he weren't so observant, that Dora mightn't be in the flummox she is now.

Dan (*cheerfully*): That's true, ma'am.

Olivia (*rising*): You don't sound very repentant.

Dan (*as she crosses, stiffly*): Well, what's done's done's my motto, isn't it?

> *She goes into the sun-room. He makes a grimace after her and holds his left hand out, the thumb pointing downward.*

Mrs Bramson: And what does that mean?

Dan: She's a nice bit of ice for next summer, isn't she?

Mrs Bramson: You're a proper one to talk about next summer when Dora there'll be up hill and down dale with a perambulator. Now look here, young man, immorality——

> Mrs Terence *comes in from the kitchen.*

Mrs Terence: The butcher wants paying. And 'e says there's men ferreting at the bottom of the garden looking for that Mrs Chalfont and do you know about it.

Mrs Bramson (*furious*): Well, they won't ferret long, not among my pampas grass!...(*Calling.*) Olivia!...Oh, that girl's never there. (*Wheeling herself furiously towards the kitchen as* Mrs Terence *makes a move to help her.*) Leave me alone. I don't want to be pushed into the nettles today thank you. . . . (*Shouting loudly as she disappears into the kitchen.*) Come out of my garden, you! Come out!

Mrs Terence (*looking towards the kitchen as* Dan *takes the stub from behind his ear and lights it*): Won't let me pay the butcher, so I won't know where she keeps 'er purse; but I do know, so put that in your pipe and smoke it!

Dan(*going to her and jabbing her playfully in the arm*): They say down at the Tallboys she got enough inside of 'er purse, too.

33

MRS TERENCE: Well, nobody's seen it open. If *you* 'ave a peep inside, young fellow, you'll go down in 'istory, that's what you'll do. (DAN *salutes her. She sniffs.*) Something's boiling over.

> *She rushes back into the kitchen as* OLIVIA *comes back from the sun-room.*

OLIVIA: Did Mrs Bramson call me, do you know?

> *A pause. He surveys her from under drooping lids, rolling his cigarette on his lower lip.*

DAN: I'm sorry. I don't know your name.

OLIVIA: Oh. (*She senses his insolence, goes self-consciously to the desk and takes out the wool.*)

DAN: Not much doin' round here for a girl, is there?

> *No answer.*

It is not a very entertaining quarter of the world for a young lady, is it?

> *He gives it up as a bad job.* DORA *comes in from the kitchen.*

DORA (*eagerly*): What did she . . . (*Confused, seeing* OLIVIA.) Oh, beg pardon, miss. . . .

> *She hurries back into the kitchen.* DAN *jerks his head after her with a laugh and looks at* OLIVIA.

OLIVIA (*arranging wool at the table*): I'm not a snob, but in case you ever call here again, I'd like to point out that though I'm employed by my aunt, I'm not quite in Dora's position.

DAN: Oh, I hope not. . . . (*She turns away, confused. He moves to her.*) Though I'll be putting it all right for Dora. I'm going to marry her. And I——

OLIVIA (*coldly*): I don't believe you.

DAN (*after a pause*): You don't like me, do you?

OLIVIA: No.

DAN (*with a smile*): Well, everybody else does!

OLIVIA (*absorbed in her wool-sorting*): Your eyes are set quite wide apart, your hands are quite good . . . I don't really know what's wrong with you.

> DAN *looks at his outspread hands. A pause. He breaks it and goes nearer to her.*

DAN (*persuasively*): You know, I've been looking at you, too. You're lonely, aren't you? I could see——

OLIVIA: I'm sorry, it's a waste of time doing your stuff with me. I'm not the type. (*Crossing to the desk and turning suddenly to him.*) Are you playing up to Mrs Bramson?

DAN: Playin' up?

OLIVIA: It crossed my mind for a minute. You stand a pretty poor chance there, you know.

DAN (*after a pause, smiling*): What d'you bet me?

> OLIVIA *turns from him, annoyed, and puts the wool away.* MRS BRAMSON *careers in from the kitchen in her chair.*

MRS BRAMSON: They say they've got permits to look for that silly woman – who are *they*, I'd like to know? If there's anything I hate, it's these men who think they've got authority.

OLIVIA: I don't think they're quite as bad as men who think they've got charm. (*She goes back into the sun-room.* DAN *whistles.*)

MRS BRAMSON: What did she mean by that?

DAN: Well, it's no good her thinkin' *she's* got any, is it?

MRS BRAMSON (*sternly*): Now, young man, what about Dora? I——

DAN: Wait a minute. . . . (*Putting his hat on the table and going to her.*) Are you sure you're comfortable like that? Don't you think, Mrs Bramson, you ought to be facin' . . . a wee bit more this side, towards the sun more, eh? (*He moves her chair round till she is in the centre of the room, facing the sun-room.*) You're looking pale you know. (*As she stares at him, putting the stub in an ash-tray on the table.*) I am sorry. Excuse rudeness. . . . Another thing, Mrs Bramson – you don't mind me sayin' it, do you? – but you ought to have a rug, you know. This October weather's very treacherous.

MRS BRAMSON (*blinking*): Pale? Did you say pale?

DAN: Washed out. (*His wiles fully turned on, but not over-done in the slightest.*) The minute I saw you just now, I said to myself – now there's a lady that's got a lot to contend with.

MRS BRAMSON: Oh . . . Well, I have. Nobody knows it better than me.

DAN: No, I'm sure. . . . Oh, it must be terrible to watch everybody else striding up and down enjoying every-thing, and to see everybody tasting the fruit——

> *As she looks at him, appreciation of what he is saying grows visibly in her face.*

I'm sorry. . . . (*Diffidently.*) I didn't ha' ought to say that.

MRS BRAMSON: But it's true! As true as you are my witness, and nobody else—— (*Pulling herself together.*) Now look here, about that girl——

DAN: Excuse me a minute. . . . (*Examining her throat, like a doctor.*) Would you mind sayin' something?

MRS BRAMSON (*taken aback*): What d'you want me to say?

DAN: Yes . . .

MRS BRAMSON: Yes. What?

DAN: There's a funny twitching in your neck when you talk – very slight, of course – nerves, I expect—— But I hope your doctor knows all about it. . . . D'you mind if I ask what your ailments are?

MRS BRAMSON: . . . Hadn't you better sit down?

DAN (*sitting*): Thank you.

MRS BRAMSON: Well, I have the most terrible palpitations. I——

DAN: Palpitation? (*Whistling.*) But the way you get about!

MRS BRAMSON: Oh?

DAN: It's a pretty bad thing to have, you know. D'you know that nine women out of ten in your position'd be just sittin' down giving way?

MRS BRAMSON: Would they?

DAN: Yes, they would! I do know, as a matter of fact. I've known people with palpitations. Somebody very close to me. . . . (*After a pause, soberly.*) They're dead now. . . .

MRS BRAMSON (*startled*): Oh!

DAN: My mother, as a matter of fact. . . . (*With finely controlled emotion, practically indistinguishable from the real thing.*) I can just remember her.

MRS BRAMSON: Oh?

DAN: She died when I was six. I know that, because my dad died two years before that.

MRS BRAMSON (*vaguely*): Oh.

DAN (*studying her*): As a matter o' fact——

MRS BRAMSON: Yes?

DAN: Oh, no, it's a daft thing——

MRS BRAMSON (*the old tart note creeping back*): Come along now! Out with it!

DAN: It's only fancy, I suppose . . . but . . . you remind me a bit of her.

MRS BRAMSON: Of your mother? (*As he nods simply, her sentimentality stirring.*) Oh . . .

DAN: Have *you* got a son?

MRS BRAMSON (*self-pityingly*): I haven't anybody at all.

DAN: Oh . . . But I don't like to talk too much about my mother. (*Putting a finger unobtrusively to his eye.*) Makes me feel . . . sort of sad. . . . (*With a sudden thought.*) She had the same eyes very wide apart as you, and – and the same very good hands.

MRS BRAMSON (*looking interestedly at her fingers*): Oh? . . . And the same palpitations?

DAN: And the same palpitations. You don't mind me talking about your health, do you?

MRS BRAMSON: No.

DAN: Well, d'you know you ought to get used to letting *other* people do things for you.

MRS BRAMSON (*a great truth dawning on her*): Yes!

DAN: You ought to be *very* careful.

MRS BRAMSON: Yes! (*After a pause, eyeing him as he smiles at her.*) You're a funny boy to be a page-boy.

DAN (*shyly*): D'you think so?

MRS BRAMSON: Well, now I come to talk to you, you seem so much better class – I mean, you know so much of the world.

DAN: I've knocked about a good bit, you know. Never had any advantages, but I always tried to do the right thing.

MRS BRAMSON (*patronisingly*): I think you deserve better—— (*Sharply again.*) Talking of the right thing, what about Dora?

DAN (*disarming*): Oh, I know I'm to blame; I'm not much of a chap, but I'd put things straight like a shot if I had any money. . . . But, you see, I work at the Tallboys, get thirty bob a week, with tips – but listen to me botherin' you with my worries and rubbish the state you're in . . . well!

MRS BRAMSON: No! I can stand it.

OLIVIA *comes back from the sun-room.*
(*Pursing her lips, reflectively.*) I've taken a liking to you.

DAN: Well. . . . (*Looking round at* OLIVIA.) That's very kind of you, Mrs Bramson.

MRS BRAMSON: It's the way you talked about your mother. That's what it was.

DAN: Was it?

OLIVIA (*at the left window*): Shall I pack these books?

DAN (*going to her with alacrity, taking the parcel from her*): I'll post them for you.

OLIVIA: Oh . . .

DAN: I'm passing Shepperley post office on the bike before post time tomorrow morning. With pleasure!

MRS BRAMSON: Have you got to go back?

DAN: Now? Well no, not really . . . I've finished my duty now I done that errand, and this is my half-day.

MRS BRAMSON (*imperiously*): Stay to lunch.

DAN (*apparently taken aback, after a look at* OLIVIA): Well – I don't like to impose myself——

MRS BRAMSON: In the kitchen, of course.

DAN: Oh, I know——

MRS BRAMSON: There's plenty of food! Stay to lunch!

DAN: Well – I don't know . . . all right, so long as you let me help a bit this morning. . . . Don't you want some string for this? Where's it kep'?

MRS BRAMSON: That woman knows. In the kitchen somewhere.

DAN: Through here?

　　He tosses the books on the sofa and hurries into the kitchen. MRS BRAMSON *holds out her hands and studies them with a new interest.*

MRS BRAMSON: That boy's got understanding.

OLIVIA: Enough to marry Dora?

MRS BRAMSON: You ought to learn to be a little less bitter, my dear. Never hook a man if you don't. With him and that Dora, I'm not so sure it wasn't six of one and half a dozen of the other. I know human nature, and mark my words, that boy's going to do big things.

A scurry in the garden. MRS TERENCE *rushes in from the front door, madly excited.*

MRS TERENCE: The paper-boy's at the back gate, and says there's a placard in Shepperley, and it's got 'News of the World – Shepperley Mystery' on it!

MRS BRAMSON: What!

OLIVIA: They've got it in the papers!

MRS TERENCE: They've got it in the papers! D'ye want any? (*Beside herself.*)

MRS BRAMSON: Catch him quick!

MRS TERENCE: First time I ever 'eard of Shepperley being in print before – hi! (*She races out of the front door.*)

MRS BRAMSON: Running around the house shouting like a lunatic! Sensation mad! Silly woman!

DORA *runs in from kitchen.*

DORA: They've got it in the papers!

MRS BRAMSON: Go away!

MRS TERENCE (*off*): I've bought three!

MRS BRAMSON (*shouting*): Be QUIET!

MRS TERENCE *runs back with three Sunday newspapers and gives one to* OLIVIA *and one to* MRS BRAMSON.

OLIVIA (*sitting left of the table*): I expect it is a bit of an event.

MRS TERENCE (*leaning over the table, searching in her paper*): 'E says they're selling like ninepins——

MRS BRAMSON (*turning pages over, impatiently*): Where *is* it? . . .

MRS TERENCE: Oh, I expect it's nothink after all. . . .

OLIVIA: Here it is. . . . (*Reading.*) 'Disappeared mysteriously . . . woods round the village being searched' . . . then her description . . . tall . . . blonde. . . .

MRS TERENCE: Blonde? I should think she is . . . I can't find it!

OLIVIA: Here's something . . . 'A keeper in the Shepperley woods was closely questioned late last night, but he has heard nothing, beyond a woman's voice in the woods on the afternoon in question, and a man's voice, probably with her, singing "Mighty Lak a Rose". Inquiries are being pursued. . . .'

MRS BRAMSON: 'Mighty Lak a Rose'. What rubbish! . . .

MRS TERENCE: Oh yes. . . . It's the 'eadline in this one. (*Humming the tune absently as she reads.*) 'Don't know what to call you, but you're mighty lak a rose.' . . . Those men have done rummaging in the garden, anyway.

MRS BRAMSON: I must go this minute and have a look at my pampas grass. And if they've damaged it I'll bring an action.

MRS TERENCE: Fancy Shepperley bein' in print——

MRS BRAMSON: Wheel me out, and don't talk so much.

MRS TERENCE (*manœuvring her through the front door*): I could talk me 'ead off and not talk as much as some people I could mention.

> OLIVIA *is alone. A pause. She spreads her paper on the table and finds* DAN's *hat under it. She picks it up and looks at it;* DAN *comes in from the kitchen with a ball of tangled string, a cigarette between his lips. He is about to take the books into the kitchen, when he sees her. He crosses to her.*

DAN: Excuse me. . . . (*Taking the hat from her, cheerfully.*) I think I'll hang it in the hall, same as if I was a visitor. . . . (*He does so, then takes up the books, sits on the sofa, and begins*

41

to unravel the string. A pause.) You don't mind me stayin' and havin' a bit o' lunch . . . in the kitchen, do you?

OLIVIA: It's not for me to say. As I told you before I'm really a servant here.

DAN (*after a pause*): You're not a very ordinary servant, though, are you?

OLIVIA (*turning over a page*): N-no. . . .

DAN: Neither am I.

> *He unpicks a knot, and begins to hum absent-mindedly. The humming gradually resolves itself into faint singing.*

(*Singing.*) 'I'm a pretty little feller . . . everybody knows. . . .'

> OLIVIA *looks up; a thought crosses her mind. She turns her head and looks at him. The curtain begins to fall slowly.*

(*Singing, as he intently unravels the string.*) 'Don't know what to call me – but I'm mighty lak a rose. . . .'

THE CURTAIN IS DOWN

ACT II

SCENE I

An afternoon twelve days later. The weather is a little duller.
    MRS BRAMSON *is sitting on the right of the table in her invalid chair, puzzling out a game of patience. She has smartened up her appearance in the interval and is wearing purple, and ear-rings.* OLIVIA *is sitting opposite her, smoking a cigarette, a pencil and pad on the table in front of her; and is pondering and writing. A portable gramophone on a small table next the desk is playing the H.M.V. dance record of 'Dames', or any jaunty tune with suitable words.*
    A pause. MRS BRAMSON *coughs. She coughs again, and looks at* OLIVIA, *waving her hand before her, clearing away billows of imaginary smoke.*

OLIVIA: I'm sorry. Is my cigarette worrying you?
MRS BRAMSON (*temper*): Not at all. I like it!
    OLIVIA *stubs out her cigarette with a resigned look and goes on making notes.* DAN *enters from the kitchen, keeping time to the music, carrying a bunch of roses, wearing overalls over flannel trousers and a brown golf jacket, and smoking. He goes to the fireplace and clumps the roses into a vase on the mantelpiece, humming the tune. He crosses to the gramophone, still in rhythm,* MRS BRAMSON *keeping time skittishly with her hands. He turns the gramophone and looks over* OLIVIA'S *shoulder at what she is writing.*
DAN (*singing*): 'Their home addresses . . . and their

43

caresses . . . linger in my memory of . . . those beautiful dames' . . . (*His hand to his forehead.*) That's me!

> OLIVIA *looks at him coldly and continues her notes.*

MRS BRAMSON: It won't come out. . . .

> DAN *shrugs his shoulders, stands behind* MRS BRAM-SON's *chair, and studies her play.* OLIVIA *follows his example from her side.*

OLIVIA (*pointing to two cards*): Look.

MRS BRAMSON (*infuriated*): I saw that! Leave me alone, and don't interfere.

> *A pause,* DAN *makes a quick movement and puts one card on another.*

(*Pleased and interested, quite unconscious of the difference in her attitude.*) Oh yes, dear, of course.

OLIVIA (*as* MRS BRAMSON *makes a move*): No, that's a spade.

MRS BRAMSON (*sharply*): No such thing; it's a club. It's got a wiggle on it.

DAN: They both got wiggles on 'em. (*Pointing to another card.*) This is a club.

MRS BRAMSON: Oh, yes, dear, so it is!

OLIVIA (*writing*): The ironmonger says there *were* two extra gallons of paraffin not paid for.

MRS BRAMSON: And they *won't* be paid for either – not if I have to go to law about it. (*A pause. She coughs absently.*)

DAN: I'm sorry. Is my cigarette worrying you!

MRS BRAMSON: Oh no, dear.

> *This has its effect on* OLIVIA. DAN *sits on the left of the table, where 'East Lynne' is open on the table.*

MRS BRAMSON: I'm sick of patience.

DAN (*reading laboriously*): 'You old-fashioned child——'

MRS BRAMSON: What?

DAN: *East Lynne.*

MRS BRAMSON: Oh . . .

DAN (*reading*): ' "You old-fashioned child!" retorted Mrs Vane, "Why did you not put on your diamonds?" "I – did – put on my diamonds," stay-mered Lady Isabel. "But I – took them off again." "What on earth for?" ' That's the other lady speaking there——

MRS BRAMSON: Yes dear. . . .

DAN: ' "What on earth for?" . . . "I did not like to be too fine," answered Lady Isabel, with a laugh' – (*turning over*) – 'and a blush. "They glittered so! I feared it might be thought I had put them on to look fine." '

MRS BRAMSON (*absently*): Good, isn't it?

DAN (*flicking ash*): Oh, yes, realistic. . . . (*Reading.*) " 'I see you mean to set up among that class of people who pree-tend to dee-spise ornyment," scornfully ree-marked Mrs Vane. "It is the ree-finement of aff-affectation, Lady Isabel——" '

> *An excited knock at the kitchen door.* DORA *enters.* DAN *turns back the page and surveys what he has been reading, scratching his head.*

MRS BRAMSON (*the old edge to her voice*): What is it?

DORA: Them men's in the wood again.

MRS BRAMSON: What men?

DORA: The men lookin' for that Mrs Chalfont.

> *A pause.* DAN *hums under his breath.*

MRS BRAMSON: You don't mean to tell me they're still at it? But they've been pottering about since . . . when was that day Mr Dan left the Tallboys?

DORA (*stressing a little bitterly*): *Mister* Dan?

DAN (*smiling*): Ahem! . . .

DORA: *Mister* Dan first came to work for you, mum, a week last Monday. . . .

MRS BRAMSON: Well, I think it's a disgrace——

DORA: *I've* found something!

DAN'S humming stops abruptly; he swivels round and looks at DORA, *his face unseen by the audience.* OLIVIA *and* MRS BRAMSON *stare at* DORA; *a pause.*

MRS BRAMSON: *You've* found something?

OLIVIA: What?

DORA (*excitedly*): This!

She holds out her left arm and lets fall from her fist the length of a soiled belt. A pause. OLIVIA *puts down her pencil and pad, goes to her, and looks at the belt.*

OLIVIA: Yes, of course, it's mine! I missed it last week. . . .

MRS BRAMSON (*baulked of excitement*): Oh yes, I thought I recognised it. . . . What nonsense! . . .

DAN looks at her chuckling.

DORA (*going, dolefully*): I'm ever so disappointed. . . .

She goes into the kitchen. OLIVIA *goes to the arm-chair by the fireplace.*

MRS BRAMSON: She'll be joining Scotland Yard next . . . Go on, dear.

DAN (*reading*): ' "It is the ree-finement of affectation, Lady Isabel——" ' (*The clock chimes. Clapping his hands, to* MRS BRAMSON.) Ah!

MRS BRAMSON (*pleased*): Oh, Danny. . . .

He hurries to the medicine cupboard and pours medicine into a spoon. HUBERT *comes in from the front door.*

HUBERT (*eagerly*): Have you heard?

MRS BRAMSON (*eagerly*): What?

HUBERT: Dora's found a belt!

MRS BRAMSON (*disappointed again*): Oh. . . . It was Olivia's.

HUBERT: I say, what a shame! . . .

MRS BRAMSON: Tch, tch! . . . All this sensation-mong—— (DAN *drowns her speech by deftly pouring the spoonful of medicine down her throat. He pushes her chocolate-box towards her, and strides briskly into the hall.*) Horrid. . . .

DAN (*taking a soft hat from the rack and putting it on*): Good for you, though, the way you are. . . .

MRS BRAMSON: Yes, dear.

DAN (*coming into the room, and beginning to take off his overalls.*) And now it's time for your walk. . . . (*Smiling at* OLIVIA.) It's all right, I got trousers on. . . . (*Peeling the overalls over his feet and tossing them on to the left window-seat.*) Listen to me talking about your walk, when you'll be in a chair all the time. . . . (*Chuckling, to* HUBERT.) That's funny, isn't it! . . . (*Going to* MRS BRAMSON.) Come on, I got your shawl and your rug in the hall. . . .

MRS BRAMSON (*as he wheels her into the hall*): Have you got my pills?

DAN: I got them in my pocket.

MRS BRAMSON: And my chocolates?

DAN: I got them in my pocket, too. Here's your hat – better put it on yourself.

MRS BRAMSON: Yes, dear.

DAN: And here's your shawl.

MRS BRAMSON: It isn't a shawl, it's a cape.

DAN: Well, I don't know, do I? And I carry your rug on my shoulder. . . . (*To the others.*) See you later! Be good!

> *Shutting the front door, his voice dying, as the chair passes the left window.*

Down this way today. . . .

> *A pause.* HUBERT *and* OLIVIA *look at each other.*

OLIVIA (*suddenly*): What do *you* think of him?

HUBERT (*a little taken aback*): Him? Grannie's white-headed boy, you mean? Oh, he's all right. (*Heavily.*) A bit slow in the uptake, of course. I wish he'd occasionally take that fag-end out of his mouth.

OLIVIA: He does. For *her*.

HUBERT: That's true. That's why he's made such a hit with her. Funny I haven't been able to manage it. In two weeks too ... it's uncanny.

OLIVIA: Uncanny? ... I think it's clever.

HUBERT: You don't think he's a wrong 'un, do you?

OLIVIA: What do we know about him?

HUBERT: Why ... his Christian name——

OLIVIA: And that's all.

HUBERT: He looks pretty honest.

OLIVIA: Looks? (*After a pause.*) It's rather frightening to think what a face can hide ... I sometimes catch sight of one looking at me. Careful lips, and blank eyes. ... And then I find I'm staring at myself in the glass ... and I realise how successfully I'm hiding the thoughts I know so well ... and then I know we're all ... strangers. What's behind *his* eyes? (*After a pause, with a smile.*) You're quite right, it *is* morbid.

HUBERT: D'you think he's a thief or something? By Jove, I left my links on the wash-stand before lunch——

OLIVIA: He's acting ... every minute of the time. I know he is! But he's acting pretty well, because I don't know *how* I know. ... He's walking about here all day, and talking a little, and smiling, and smoking cigarettes. ... Impenetrable ... that's what it is! What's going on – in his mind? What's he thinking of? (*Vehemently.*) He *is* thinking of something! All the time. What is it?

> DAN *enters from the front door and smiles broadly at them.*

DAN: Anybody seen my lady's pills? It's a matter of life and death ... I thought I had 'em.

HUBERT *chuckles.*

OLIVIA (*after a pause, in a level voice*): Oh yes. They're in the top drawer of the desk. I'm so sorry.

DAN: Thank you. (*He salutes her, goes to the desk, and takes out the pills. They watch him.*)

MRS BRAMSON (*off*): Danny!

HUBERT (*to say something*): Is she feeling off colour again?

DAN (*on his way to the front door*): Off colour? She'd never been on it, man! To hear her go on you'd think the only thing left is artificial respiration. *And* chocolates. . . . (*Laughing and calling.*) Coming! (*He goes, shutting the front door behind him.*)

HUBERT: No, really, you have to laugh!

OLIVIA: But what you've just seen . . . that's exactly what I mean! It's acting! He's not being himself for a minute – it's all put on for our benefit . . . don't you see?

HUBERT (*banteringly*): D'you know, I think you're in love with him.

OLIVIA (*with rather more impatience than is necessary*): Don't be ridiculous.

HUBERT: I was only joking.

OLIVIA: He's common and insolent, and I dislike him intensely.

MRS TERENCE *comes in from the kitchen.*

MRS TERENCE: What'll you 'ave for tea, scones or crumpets? Can't make both.

OLIVIA: What *d'you* think of Dan?

MRS TERENCE: Dan? Oh, 'e's all right. Bit of a mystery.

HUBERT: Oh.

MRS TERENCE (*shutting the kitchen door and coming into the middle of the room*): Terrible liar, o' course. But then a lot of us are. Told me he used to 'unt to 'ounds and 'ave

'is own pack. Before 'e went up in the world and went as
a page-boy I suppose.

OLIVIA (*to* HUBERT): You see? He wouldn't try that
on with us, but couldn't resist it with her.

HUBERT: I wonder how soon the old girl'll get his
number? . . . Oh, but fair play, we're talking about the
chap as if he were the most terrible——

MRS TERENCE: Why, what's 'e done?

HUBERT: Exactly.

OLIVIA: I don't know, but I feel so strongly. . . . Is
Dora there? . . . (*Calling cautiously.*) Dora!

MRS TERENCE: Oh, she won't know anything. She's
as 'alf-witted as she's lazy, and that's sayin' a lot. She'd
cut 'er nose off to stop the dust-bin smelling sooner than
empty it, she would.

    DORA *comes in from the kitchen, wiping her hands on*
    her apron.

DORA: Did somebody say Dora?

OLIVIA: Has Dan said any more about marrying you?

DORA: No. *She* 'asn't brought it up again, either.

OLIVIA: Does he talk to you at all?

DORA (*perplexed*): Oh . . . only how-do-you-do and
beg-your-pardon. I've never really spent any time in 'is
company, you see. Except, o' course——

HUBERT: Quite. What's your idea of him?

DORA: Oh . . . (*Moving to the centre of the room.*) 'E's all
right. Takes 'is fun where 'e finds it. And leaves it. . . .
Cracks 'imself up, you know. Pretends 'e doesn't care a
twopenny, but always got 'is eye on what you're thinking
of 'im . . . if you know what I mean.

OLIVIA: Yes, I do. That incredible vanity . . . they
always have it. Always.

HUBERT: Who? (*A pause.*)

OLIVIA: Murderers.

A pause. They stare at her.

HUBERT: Good God! . . .

MRS TERENCE: D'you mean . . . this woman they're looking for?

OLIVIA: I'm sure of it.

MRS TERENCE: But 'e's such a – such a ordinary boy——

OLIVIA: That's just it – and then he's suddenly so . . . extraordinary. I've felt it ever since I heard him sing that song – I told you——

HUBERT: That 'mighty-lak-a-rose' thing, you mean? Oh, but it's a pretty well-known one——

OLIVIA: It's more than that. I've kept on saying to myself: No, murder's a thing we read about in the papers; it isn't real life; it can't touch us . . . but it can. And it's here. All round us. In the forest . . . in this house. We're . . . living with it. (*After a pause, rising decisively.*) Bring his luggage in here, will you, Mrs Terence?

MRS TERENCE (*staggered*): 'Is luggage? (*Recovering, to* DORA.) Give me a 'and. (*Wide-eyed, she goes into the kitchen, followed by* DORA.)

HUBERT: I say, this is a bit thick, you know – spying——

OLIVIA (*urgently*): We may never have the house to ourselves again.

She runs to each window and looks across the forest.
MRS TERENCE *returns carrying luggage; one large and one small suitcase.* DORA *follows, lugging an old-fashioned thick leather hat-box.* MRS TERENCE *places the suitcase on the table;* DORA *plants the hat-box in the middle of the floor.*

MRS TERENCE (*in a conspiratorial tone*): This is all.

HUBERT: But look here, we can't do this——

OLIVIA *snaps open the lid of the larger suitcase with a jerk. A pause. They look, almost afraid.* DORA *moves to the back of the table.*

MRS TERENCE (*as* OLIVIA *lifts it gingerly*): A dirty shirt. . . .

HUBERT: That's all right.

OLIVIA: A clean pair of socks . . . packet of razor-blades. . . .

HUBERT: We shouldn't be doing this – I feel as if I were at school again.

MRS TERENCE: Singlet. . . .

OLIVIA: Half ticket to Shepperley Palais de Danse. . . .

MRS TERENCE: Oh, it's a proper 'aunt!

DORA: Oh, 'ere's a pocket-book. With a letter. (*She gives the letter to* MRS TERENCE *and the pocket-book to* OLIVIA.)

HUBERT: Look here, this is going a bit too far – you can't do this to a chap——

MRS TERENCE (*taking the letter from the envelope*): Don't be silly, dear, your wife'll do it to you 'undreds of times. . . . (*Sniffing the notepaper.*) Pooh . . . (*Reading, as they crane over her shoulder.*) 'Dear Baby-Face my own . . .' Signed Lil. . . .

OLIVIA: What awful writing. . . .

MRS TERENCE (*reading, heavily*): '. . . Next time you strike Newcastle, O.K. by me, baby. . . .' Ooh!

HUBERT: Just another servant-girl. . . . Sorry, Dora. . . .

DORA (*lugubriously*): O.K.

OLIVIA (*rummaging in the pocket-book*): Bus ticket to Thorburton, some snaps. . . .

MRS TERENCE: Look at 'er *bust*!

OLIVIA: Here's a group. . . . Look, Hubert. . . .

HUBERT *joins her in front of the table.*

HUBERT: This wench is rather fetching.

MRS TERENCE (*coming between them*): Look at 'er! . . The impudence, 'er being taken in a bathing suit! . . .

DORA: He's not in this one, is 'e?

HUBERT (*impressed*): Oh, I say . . . there *she* is!

MRS TERENCE: ⎱ Who?
DORA: ⎰

HUBERT: The missing female! In front of the tall man. . . You remember the photograph of her in the *Mirror*?

DORA: It's awful to think she may be dead. Awful. . . .

MRS TERENCE: Looks ever so sexy, doesn't she?

DORA: 'Ere's one of a little boy——

OLIVIA: How extraordinary. . . .

HUBERT: What?

OLIVIA: It's himself.

DORA: The little Eton collar. . . . Oh dear . . . ever so sweet, isn't it?

MRS TERENCE: Now that's what I call a real innocent face. . . .

HUBERT (*going to the centre of the room*): Well, that's that. . . .

OLIVIA: Wait a minute, wasn't there another one? (*Seeing the hat-box.*) Oh yes. . . .

HUBERT (*lifting it on to the chair*): Oh, this; yes. . . .

DORA: Old-fashioned, isn't it?

MRS TERENCE: I should think he got it from a box-room at the Tallboys——

OLIVIA (*puzzled*): But it looks extraordinary—— (*She gives a sudden gasp. They look at her. She is staring at the box. A pause.*)

HUBERT: What is it?

OLIVIA: I don't know. . . . Suppose there is something . . . inside it?

A pause. They stare at her, fascinated by her thought. The front door bangs. They are electrified into action; but it is too late. It is DAN. *He goes briskly to the table.*

DAN: She wants to sit in the sun now and have a bit of *East Lynne.* Talk about changin' her mind——

He sees the suitcase on the table before him, and is motionless and silent. A pause. The others dare not move. He finally breaks the situation, takes up 'East Lynne' from the table, and walks slowly back to the front door. He stops, looks at HUBERT, *smiles and comes down to him. His manner is normal – too normal.*

Could I have it back, please? It's the only one I got. . . .

HUBERT: Oh . . . yes, of course. . . . (*Handing him the pocket-book.*)

DAN (*taking it*): Thank you very much.

HUBERT: Not at all . . . I . . . (*To* OLIVIA.) Here, you deal with this. It's beyond me.

DAN (*to him*): Did you see the picture of me when I was a little fellow?

HUBERT: Yes . . . Very jolly.

DAN (*turning to* MRS TERENCE): Did *you*? It was in the inside of my wallet.

MRS TERENCE: Oh . . . was it?

DAN: Yes. Where I should be keeping my money, only any bit of money I have I always keep *on* me. (*Turning to* HUBERT.) Safer, don't you think?

HUBERT (*smiling weakly*): Ye'es. . . .

DAN: I only keep one ten-bob note in this wallet, for emergencies. . . . (*Looking.*) That's funny, it's gone. (*He looks at* HUBERT. *The others look blankly at one another.*) . . .

I expect I dropped it somewhere . . . what did you think of the letter?

HUBERT: Letter?

DAN: You got it in your hand.

HUBERT: Well, I didn't – er——

DAN: Means well, does Lil; but we had a row. (*Taking back the letter.*) She would spy on me. And if there's anything I hate, it's spyin'. Don't you agree?

HUBERT: Ye'es.

DAN: I'd sooner have anything than a spy. (*To* MRS TERENCE.) Bar a murderer, o' course.

    A pause. He is arranging his property in his wallet.

HUBERT (*incredulous*): What – what did you say?

DAN (*turning to him, casually*): Bar a murderer, o' course.

    OLIVIA *steps forward.* MRS TERENCE *steps back from the chair on which the hat-box has been placed.*

OLIVIA (*incisively*): Talking of murder, do you know anything about Mrs Chalfont's whereabouts at the moment?

    DAN *turns to her, and for the first time sees the hat-box. He stands motionless. A pause.*

DAN: Mrs Who?

OLIVIA: You can't pretend you've never heard of her.

DAN (*turning to* HUBERT, *recovering himself*): Oh, Mrs *Chalfont's* whereabouts! I thought she said her name was Mrs Chalfontswear. (*Profusely.*) Silly. . . . Swear – about – couldn't think——

OLIVIA: Well?

DAN (*still looking at* HUBERT, *brightly after a pause*): I've nothin' to go on, but I think she's been . . . murdered.

HUBERT: Oh, you do?

DAN: Yes, I do.

MRS TERENCE: Who by?

DAN: They say she had several chaps on a string, and—— (*Suddenly.*) There was one fellow, a London chap, a bachelor, very citified – with a fair moust—— (*He stares at* HUBERT.)

HUBERT (*touching his moustache, unconsciously*): What are you looking at me for?

DAN: Well . . . you wasn't round these parts the day she bunked, was you?

HUBERT: Yes, I was, as a matter of fact.

DAN (*significantly*): Oh. . . .

MRS BRAMSON'S VOICE (*calling in the garden*): Danny!

HUBERT(*flustered*): What in God's name are you getting at?

> DAN *smiles, shrugs his shoulders regretfully at him, and goes out through the front door.* OLIVIA *sits at the table.*

MRS TERENCE (*to* HUBERT, *perplexed*): Are you *sure* you didn't do it, sir?

HUBERT: I'm going out for a breath of air. (*He takes his hat and stick as he goes through the hall, and goes out through the front door.*)

MRS TERENCE (*to* OLIVIA): You don't still think——

OLIVIA: I won't say any more. I know how silly it sounds.

> DORA *runs into the kitchen, snivelling.*

MRS TERENCE (*to* OLIVIA): The way you worked us all up. Doesn't it all go to show——

> *She hears* DAN *return, and looks round apprehensively. He goes to the table slowly and looks at the two suitcases.*

DAN (*smiling to* MRS TERENCE): Would you mind please givin' me a hand with the tidyin' up. . . . (*Taking up the suitcases.*) And carryin' the other one? . . . (*Going into the kitchen, followed by* MRS TERENCE *carrying the hat-box.*) Looks as if we're goin' on our holidays, doesn't it? . . .

> OLIVIA *is alone for a moment. She stares before her, perplexed.* DAN *returns. She looks away. He looks at her, his eyes narrowed. A pause. Studying her, he takes from the pocket of his jacket a formidable-looking clasp-knife, unclasps it, and tests the blade casually with his fingers. He glances at the mantelpiece, crosses to it, takes down a stick and begins to sharpen the end of it.* OLIVIA *watches him. A pause.*

OLIVIA: Did you do it?

> *He whittles at the stick.*

DAN: You wouldn't be bad-lookin' without them glasses.

OLIVIA: It doesn't interest me very much what I look like.

DAN: Don't you believe it. . . . (*Surveying the shavings in the hearth.*) Tch! . . . Clumsy. . . . *Looking round and seeing a newspaper lying on the table.*) Ah. . . . (*Crossing to the table, then smiling, with the suspicion of a mock-bow.*) Excuse me. . . . (*He unfolds the newspaper on the table and begins to whittle the stick over it.*)

OLIVIA: You're very conceited, aren't you?

DAN (*reassuringly*): Yes. . . .

OLIVIA: And you *are* acting all the time, aren't you?

DAN (*staring at her, as if astonished*): Actin'? Actin' what? (*Leaning over the table, on both arms.*) Look at the way I can look you in the eyes. I'll stare you out. . . .

OLIVIA (*staring into his eyes*): I have a theory it's the criminals who *can* look you in the eyes, and the honest people who blush and look away.

DAN (*smiling*): Oh. . . .

OLIVIA (*after a pause, challenging*): It's a very blank
look, though, isn't it?

DAN (*smiling*): Is it?

OLIVIA: You *are* acting, aren't you?

DAN (*after a pause, in a whisper, almost joyfully*): Yes!

OLIVIA (*fascinated*): And what are you like when you
stop acting?

DAN: I dunno, it's so long since I stopped.

OLIVIA: But when you're alone?

DAN: Then I act more than ever I do.

OLIVIA: Why?

DAN: I dunno; 'cause I like it. . . . (*Breaking the scene,
pulling a chair round to the table.*) Now what d'ye say if *I*
ask a question or two for a change? (*Sitting in the chair,
facing her.*) Just for a change . . . Why can't you take a bit
of an interest in some other body but me?

OLIVIA (*taken aback*): I'm not interested in you. Only
you don't talk. That's bound to make people wonder.

DAN: I can talk a lot sometimes. A drop o' drink makes
a power o' difference to me. (*Chuckling.*) You'd be surprised. . . . Ah. . . . (*He returns to his work.*)

OLIVIA: I wonder if I would . . . .

DAN: I know you would. . . .

OLIVIA: I think I can diagnose you all right.

DAN: Carry on.

OLIVIA: You haven't any feelings . . . at all. . . .

He looks slowly up at her. She has struck home.

But you live in a world of your own. . . . A world of
your own imagination.

DAN: I don't understand so very well, not bein' so very
liter-er-airy.

OLIVIA: You follow me perfectly well.

He shrugs his shoulders, laughs, and goes on whittling.

DAN: D'you still think there's been a bit o' dirty work?

OLIVIA: I don't know what to think now. I suppose not.

DAN (*intent on his work, his back to the audience*): Disappointed?

OLIVIA: What on earth do you mean?

DAN: Disappointed?

OLIVIA (*laughing, in spite of herself*): Yes, I suppose I am.

DAN: Why?

OLIVIA (*the tension at last relaxed*): Oh, I don't know. . . . Because nothing much has ever happened to me, and it's a dull day, and it's the depths of the country. . . . I don't know. . . .

> *A piercing scream from the bottom of the garden. A pause.*

MRS BRAMSON (*shrieking, from the other side of the house*): Danny! . . . Danny!

> *The clatter of footsteps in the garden.* DORA *runs in from the hall, breathless and terrified.*

DORA: They're diggin' . . . in the rubbish-pit. . . .

OLIVIA: Well?

DORA: There's something sticking out. . . .

OLIVIA: What?

DORA: A hand. . . . Somebody's hand! . . . Oh, Miss Grayne . . . somebody's hand. . . . (*She runs whimpering into the kitchen, and* OLIVIA *rises and runs to the left window and looks out.*)

MRS BRAMSON'S VOICE (*calling off*): Danny!

> DAN *rises slowly, his back to the audience.* OLIVIA *turns and suddenly sees him. Horror grows in her face.*
> *The blare of music.*
> *The lights dim out.*

SCENE II

*The music plays in darkness for a few bars, then the curtain rises
again. The music fades away.*

    Late afternoon, two days later. OLIVIA *is seated above
the table snipping long cuttings from newspapers and past-
ing them into a ledger. A knock at the front door. She starts
nervously. Another knock.* MRS TERENCE *comes in from
the kitchen carrying a smoothing-iron.*

MRS TERENCE: If it's the police again, I'll bash their
helmets in with this. If it lands me three months, I
will.

OLIVIA: They're from Scotland Yard, and they don't
wear helmets.

MRS TERENCE: Then they're going to get 'urt. . . .
(*Going into the hall.*) I can tell by their looks what they
think. And they better not think it, neither.

OLIVIA: And what do they think?

MRS TERENCE (*over her shoulder*): They think it's me. I
know they think it's me. (*She goes into the hall and opens the
front door.*)

HUBERT (*outside*): Good afternoon, Mrs Terence.

MRS TERENCE: Oh . . . come in, sir. (*Coming back into
the room.*) It's a civilian for a change. (*She is followed by*
HUBERT.)

HUBERT (*to* OLIVIA): I say, this is all getting pretty
terrible, isn't it?

OLIVIA: Yes, terrible.

MRS TERENCE: Oh, terrible, terrible. There's one word
for it; it's terrible. Forty-eight hours since they found
'er. They'll never get 'im now.

HUBERT: Terrible.

MRS TERENCE: There was another charabanc load just after two o'clock. All standing round the rubbish 'eap eating sandwiches. Sensation, that's what it is.

OLIVIA: Would you like some food, Hubert?

HUBERT: Well, I——

MRS TERENCE: They're still looking for the 'ead.

HUBERT (*to* OLIVIA, *with a slight grimace*): No, thanks. I had lunch.

MRS TERENCE: Mangled, she was, mangled. . . . Did you see your name in the paper, sir?

HUBERT: I – er – did catch a glimpse of it, yes.

MRS TERENCE: Little did you think, sir, when you was digging that pit for my rubbish, eh? 'E may 'ave been watching you digging it . . . ooh! I have to sit in my kitchen and think about it.

HUBERT: Then why don't you leave?

MRS TERENCE (*indignantly*): How can I leave with the whole village waitin' on me to tell 'em the latest? (*Going towards the kitchen.*) I 'eard 'er 'ead must have been off at one stroke. One stroke. . . .

HUBERT: Really . . .

MRS TERENCE (*turning at the door*): She wasn't interfered with, though. (*She goes into the kitchen.*)

HUBERT: How they all love it. . . . How's the old lady bearing up in the invalid chair, eh?

OLIVIA: She's bursting out of it with health. And loving it more than anybody. This is my latest job – a press-cutting book. There was a picture of her in the *Chronicle* yesterday; she bought twenty-six copies.

HUBERT (*taking his pipe out*): She'll get to believe she did it herself in the end. . . . Is she in?

OLIVIA: She's gone over to Breakerly to interview a local paper.

HUBERT: The lad pushing the go-cart? . . . He's the devoted son all right, isn't he?

OLIVIA (*after a pause*): I don't talk to him much.

HUBERT: Nice fellow. I've thought a lot about that prying into his things – pretty bad show, you know. (*Going to the left window.*) I wonder if they'll ever nab him?

OLIVIA (*with a start*): What do you mean?

HUBERT: The fellow who did it. . . . Wonder what he's doing now.

OLIVIA: I wonder.

HUBERT: Damn clever job you know, quietly. . . . That was a rum touch, finding that broken lipstick in the rubbish-heap. . . . You know, the fact they still have no idea where this woman's head is——

OLIVIA (*convulsively*): Don't. . . .

HUBERT: Sorry.

OLIVIA (*after a pause*): It's a bit of a strain.

HUBERT (*earnestly*): Then why don't you leave?

OLIVIA: I – I couldn't afford it.

HUBERT: But you *could* if you married me! Now, look here—— (*Going to her.*) You said you'd tell me today. So here I am – er – popping the question again. There's nothing much to add, except to go over the old ground again, and say that I'm not what you'd call a terrible brainy chap, but I am straight.

OLIVIA: Yes, I know.

HUBERT: Though, again, I'm not the sort that gets into corners with a pipe, and never opens his mouth from one blessed year's end to the other. I can talk.

OLIVIA: Yes, you can.

HUBERT: An all-round chap, really – that's me.

OLIVIA: Yes.

HUBERT: Well?

OLIVIA: I'm sorry, Hubert, but I can't.

HUBERT: You can't? But you told me that day we might make a go of it, or words to that effect——

OLIVIA: I've thought it over since then, and I'm afraid I can't.

A pause.

HUBERT: What's changed you?

OLIVIA: Nothing's changed me, Hubert. I've just thought the matter over, that's all.

A pause. He crosses towards the fireplace.

HUBERT: Is it another man?

OLIVIA (*startled*): Don't be silly. (*Collecting herself.*) What man could I possibly meet cooped up here?

HUBERT: Sorry. Can't be helped. Sorry.

DAN (*in the garden*): There we are. Nice outing, eh——

OLIVIA: So am I.

> *The front door opens and* DAN *wheels in* MRS BRAM-
> SON. *He is as serene as ever, but more animated than before.*
> *He is dressed the same as in the previous scene, and is*
> *smoking his usual cigarette.* HUBERT *sits at the table.*

DAN (*hanging up her rug in the hall*): Back home again – I put your gloves away——

MRS BRAMSON (*as he wheels her in*): I feel dead. (*To* HUBERT.) Oh, it's you . . . I feel dead.

DAN (*sitting beside her on the sofa, full of high spirits*): Don't you be a silly old 'oman, you look as pretty as a picture – strawberries and cream in your face, and not a day over forty; and when I've made you a nice cup of tea you'll be twenty-five in the sun and eighteen with your back to the light, so you think yourself lucky!

MRS BRAMSON (*as he digs her in the side*): Oh, Danny, you are a terror! (*To the others.*) He's been at me like this all the way. I must say it keeps me alive.

DAN (*as she hands him her hat and cape*): But you feel dead.
I get you.

MRS BRAMSON (*kittenish*): Oh, you caution! You'll be
the death of me.

DAN (*wagging his finger at her*): Ah-ha! (*Hanging up her
things in the hall.*) Now what'd you like a drop of in your
tea – gin, whisky, liqueur brandy, or a nice dollop of
sailor's rum, eh?

MRS BRAMSON: Just listen to him! Now don't make
me laugh, dear, because there's always my heart.

DAN (*sitting beside her again*): You've lost your heart,
you know you have to the little feller that pushes your
pram – you know you have!

MRS BRAMSON (*laughing shrilly*): Pram! Well! (*Her laugh
cut short.*) It's wicked to laugh, with this – this thing all
round us.

DAN (*sobering portentously*): I forgot. (*As she shivers.*)
Not in a draught, are you? (*Shutting the front door and
coming down to* HUBERT.) D'you remember, Mr Laurie,
me, pulling your leg about you havin' done it? Funniest
thing out! . . . Talk about laugh!

MRS BRAMSON (*fondly*): Tttt! . . .

DAN (*a glint of mischief in his eyes*): I think I better get
the tea before I get into hot water. (*He goes towards the
kitchen.*)

OLIVIA: Mrs Terence is getting the tea.

DAN (*at the door*): She don't make tea like me. I'm an
old sailor, Miss Grayne. Don't you forget that. (*He goes
into the kitchen.*)

OLIVIA: I'm not interested, I'm afraid.

MRS BRAMSON (*wheeling herself to the front of the table*):
Look here, Olivia, you're down right rude to that boy,
and if there's one thing that never gets a woman any-

where, it's rudeness. What have you got against him?

HUBERT: Surely he's got more to say for himself today then when I met him before.

MRS BRAMSON: Oh, he's been in rare spirits all day.

HUBERT: Johnny Walker, judging by the whiff of breath I got just now.

MRS BRAMSON: Meaning whisky?

HUBERT: Yes.

OLIVIA: I've never heard you make a joke before, Hubert.

HUBERT: Didn't realise it was one till I'd said it. Sorry.

MRS BRAMSON: It's not a joke; it's a libel. (*A knock at the front door.*) Come in. The boy's a teetotaller.

> NURSE LIBBY *enters from the front door.*

HUBERT: Sorry, my mistake.

NURSE: Good afternoon. Shall I wait for you in your bedroom?

MRS BRAMSON: Yes. I feel absolutely dead.

NURSE (*turning at the bedroom, eagerly*): Anything new *re* the murder?

HUBERT: I believe her head was cut off at one stroke.

NURSE (*brightly*): Oh, poor thing. . . .

> *She goes into the bedroom.* DAN *returns from the kitchen, carrying a tray of tea and cakes.*

DAN: There you are, fresh as a daisy. Three lumps, as per usual, and some of the cakes you like——

MRS BRAMSON (*as he pours out her tea*): Thank you, dear. . . . Let me smell your breath. (*After smelling it.*) Clean as a whistle. Smells of peppermints.

OLIVIA: Yes. There were some in the kitchen.

HUBERT: Oh.

MRS BRAMSON (*to* HUBERT, *as* DAN *pours out two more cups*): So you won't stay to tea, Mr – er——

HUBERT: Er – (*rising*) – no thank you. . . . (DAN *sits in* HUBERT's *chair.*) I think I'll get off before it's dark. Good-bye, Mrs Bramson. Good-bye, Mr – er——

DAN (*grinning and saluting*): Dan. Just Dan. (*He opens the press-cutting ledger.*)

HUBERT (*to* OLIVIA): Good-bye.

OLIVIA (*rises*): Good-bye, Hubert. I'm sorry.

    DAN *raises his cup as if drinking a toast to* MRS BRAMSON. *She follows suit.*

HUBERT: Can't be helped. . . . It'll get dark early today, I think. Funny how the evenings draw in this time of year. Good night.

DAN: Good night.

HUBERT (*to* OLIVIA): Good-bye.

OLIVIA: Good-bye. (*She goes to the right window-seat.*)

MRS BRAMSON: Johnny Walker, indeed! Impertinence!

DAN (*drinking tea and scanning press-cuttings*): Johnny Walker?

MRS BRAMSON: Never you mind, dear. . . . Any more of those terrible people called? Reporters? Police?

DAN (*gaily*): There's a definite fallin' off in attendance today. Sunday, I expect.

MRS BRAMSON: Hush, don't talk like that, dear.

DAN: Sorry, mum.

MRS BRAMSON: And don't call me 'mum'!

DAN: Well, if I can't call you Mrs. Bramson, what can I call you.

MRS BRAMSON: If you were very good, I might let you call me . . . mother!

DAN (*mischievously, his hand to his forehead*): O.K., mother.

MRS BRAMSON (*joining in his laughter*): Oh, you are in a mood today! (*Suddenly, imperiously.*) I want to be read to, now.

DAN (*crossing to the desk in mock resignation*): Your servant, mother o' mine. . . . What'll you have? *The Channings? The Red Court Farm?*

MRS BRAMSON. I'm tired of them.

DAN: Well . . . oh! (*Taking a large Bible from the top of the desk.*) What about the Bible?

MRS BRAMSON: The Bible?

DAN: It's Sunday, you know. I was brought up to it!

MRS BRAMSON: So was I . . . *East Lynne's* nice, though.

DAN: Not so nice as the Bible.

MRS BRAMSON (*doubtfully*): All right, dear; makes a nice change. . . . Not that I don't often dip into it.

DAN: I'm sure you do. (*Blowing the dust off the book.*) Now where'll I read?

MRS BRAMSON (*unenthusiastic*): At random's nice, don't you think, dear?

DAN: At random. . . . Yes. . . .

MRS BRAMSON: The Old Testament.

DAN (*turning over leaves thoughtfully*): At random in the Old Testament's a bit risky, don't you think so?

MRS TERENCE *comes in from the kitchen.*

MRS TERENCE (*to* MRS BRAMSON): The paper-boy's at the door again and says you're in the *News of the World* again.

MRS BRAMSON (*interested*): Oh! . . . (*Simulating indifference.*) That horrible boy again, when the one thing I want is to blot the whole thing out of my mind.

MRS TERENCE: 'Ow many copies d'you want?

MRS BRAMSON: Get three.

MRS TERENCE: *And* 'e says there's a placard in Shepperley with your name on it.

MRS BRAMSON: What does it say?

MRS TERENCE: 'Mrs Bramson Talks'. (*She goes back towards the kitchen.*)

MRS BRAMSON: Oh. (*As* MRS TERENCE *reaches the kitchen door.*) Go at once into Shepperley and order some. At once!

MRS TERENCE: Can't be done.

MRS BRAMSON: Can't be done? What d'you mean, can't be done? It's a scandal. What are you paid for?

MRS TERENCE (*coming back, furious*): I'm not paid! And 'aven't been for two weeks! And I'm not coming to-morrow unless I am. Put that in your copybook and blot it. (*She goes into the kitchen, banging the door.*)

MRS BRAMSON: Isn't paid? Is she mad? (*To* OLIVIA.) Are you mad? Why don't you pay her?

OLIVIA (*coming down*): Because you don't give me the money to do it with.

MRS BRAMSON: I – (*fumbling at her bodice*) – wheel me over to that cupboard.

OLIVIA *is about to do so, when she catches* DAN's *eye.*

OLIVIA (*to* DAN *pointedly*): Perhaps *you'd* go into the kitchen and get the paper from Mrs Terence?

DAN (*after a second's pause, with a laugh*): Of course I will, madam! Anythin' you say! Anythin' you say!

He careers into the kitchen, still carrying the Bible.
MRS BRAMSON *has fished up two keys on the end of a long black tape.* OLIVIA *wheels her over to the cupboard above the fireplace.*

OLIVIA: If you give me the keys, I'll get it for you.

MRS BRAMSON: No fear! (*She unlocks the cupboard; it turns out to be a small but very substantial safe. Unlocking the safe, muttering to herself.*) Won't go into Shepperley, indeed ... never heard of such impertinence. ... (*She takes out a cash-box from among some deeds, unlocks it with the smaller key, and takes out a mass of five-pound and pound notes.*) The way these servants – what are you staring at?

OLIVIA: Isn't it rather a lot of money to have in the house?

MRS BRAMSON: 'Put not your trust in banks' is my motto, and always will be.

OLIVIA: But that's hundreds of pounds! It——

MRS BRAMSON (*handing her two notes*): D'you wonder I wouldn't let you have the key?

OLIVIA: Has ... anybody else asked you for it?

MRS BRAMSON (*locking the cash-box and putting it back in the safe*): I wouldn't let a soul touch it. Not a soul. Not even Danny. (*She snaps the safe, locks it, and slips the keys back into her bosom.*)

OLIVIA: Has *he* asked you for it?

MRS BRAMSON: It's enough to have these policemen prying, you forward girl, without——

OLIVIA (*urgently*): Please! Has he?

MRS BRAMSON: Well, he did offer to fetch some money yesterday for the dairy. But I wouldn't give him the key. Oh no!

OLIVIA: Why?

MRS BRAMSON: Do I want to see him waylaid and attacked, and my key stolen? Oh no, I told him, that key stays on me——

OLIVIA: Did he – know how much money there is in there?

MRS BRAMSON: I told him. Do you wonder I stick to the key, I said – what *is* the matter with you, all these questions?

OLIVIA: Oh, it's no use——

She goes to the arm-chair below the fireplace and sits in it. DAN *returns from the kitchen, with a copy of the 'News of the World'; the Bible tucked under his arm, a cigarette stub between his lips.*

DAN: He says they're sellin' like hot cakes! (*Handing the paper to* MRS BRAMSON.) There you are, I've found the place for you – whole page, headlines an' all. . . .

MRS BRAMSON: Oh yes. . . .

DAN *stands with one knee on the sofa, and turns over the pages of his Bible.*

(*Reading breathlessly, her back to the fireplace.*) '. . . The Victim's Past' . . . with another picture of me underneath! (*Looking closer, dashed.*) Oh, taken at Tonbridge the year before the war; really it isn't right. . . . (*To* OLIVIA, *savouring it.*) 'The Bungalow of Death! . . . Gruesome finds. . . . Fiendish murderer still at large. . . . The enigma of the missing head . . . where is it buried? . . .' Oh yes! (*She goes on reading silently to herself.*)

DAN (*suddenly in a clear voice*): '. . . Blessed is the man . . . that walketh not in the counsel of the ungodly . . . nor standeth in the way of sinners . . . nor sitteth in the seat of the scornful. . . .'

MRS BRAMSON (*impatiently*): Oh, the print's too small. . . .

DAN (*firmly*): Shall I read it to you?

MRS BRAMSON: Yes dear, do. . . .

He shuts the Bible with a bang, throws it on the sofa, and takes the paper from her. OLIVIA *watches him intently; he smiles at her slowly and brazenly as he shakes out the paper.*

DAN (*reading laboriously*): '. . . The murderer committed the crime in the forest most – in the forest, most likely strippin' beforehand——

DORA *comes in from the kitchen, and stands at the door, arrested by his reading. She is dressed in Sunday best.*

(*Reading.*) '. . . and cleansin' himself afterwards in the forest lake——

MRS BRAMSON: Tch! tch!

DAN (*reading*): '. . . He buried the body shallow in the open pit, cunnin'ly chancin' it bein' filled, which it was next day, the eleventh——' (*Nodding to* OLIVIA.) That was the day 'fore I come here. . . .

MRS BRAMSON: So it was. . . .

DAN (*reading*): 'The body was nude. Attempts had been made to . . . turn to foot of next column. . . .' (*Doing so.*) 'Attempts had been made to . . . era-eradicate fingerprints with a knife. . . .'

Far away, the tolling of village bells.

(*Reading.*) '. . . The head was severed by a skilled person, possibly a butcher. The murderer——' (*He stops suddenly, raises his head, smiles, takes the cigarette stub, puts it behind his ear, and listens.*)

OLIVIA: What's the matter?

MRS BRAMSON: Can you hear something? Oh, I'm scared.

DAN: I forgot it was Sunday. . . . They're goin' to church in the villages. All got up in their Sunday best, with prayer-books, and the organ playin', and the windows shinin'. Shinin' on holy things, because holy things isn't afraid of the daylight.

MRS BRAMSON: But Danny, what on earth are you——

DAN (*quelling her*): But all the time, the daylight's movin' over the floor, and by the end of the sermon the air in the church is turning grey. . . . And people isn't able to think of holy things so much no more, only of the terrible things that's goin' on outside, that everybody's readin' about in the papers! (*Looking at* OLIVIA.) Because they know that though it's still daylight, and everythin's

71

or'nary and quiet . . . today will be the same as all the other days, and come to an end, and it'll be night. . . . (*After a pause, coming to earth again with a laugh at the others, throwing the newspaper on the sofa.*) I forgot it was Sunday!

MRS BRAMSON (*overawed*): Good gracious . . . what's come over you, Danny?

DAN (*with exaggerated animation*): Oh, I speechify like anything when I'm roused! I used to go to Sunday School, see, and the thoughts sort of come into my head. Like as if I was reading' off a book! (*Slapping the Bible.*)

MRS BRAMSON: Dear, dear. . . . You should have been a preacher. You should!

DAN *laughs loudly and opens the Bible.*

DORA (*going to the table and collecting the tea-tray*): I never knew 'e 'ad so many words in 'is 'ead. . . .

MRS BRAMSON (*suddenly*): I want to lie down now, and be examined.

DAN (*rising*): Anything you say, mother o' mine. . . . Will you have your medicine in your room as well, eh?

MRS BRAMSON: Yes, dear. . . . Olivia, you *never* got a new bottle yesterday!

DAN (*as he wheels her into her bedroom*): I got it today while you were with the chap. . . . Popped in at the chemist's.

MRS BRAMSON: Oh, thank you, dear. The one by the mortuary? . . . Oh, my back. . . . Nurse!

Her voice is lost in the bedroom. The daylight begins to fade. The church bells die away.

DORA: My sister says all this is wearin' me to a shadow.

OLIVIA: It is trying, isn't it?

DORA: You look that worried, too, Miss Grayne.

OLIVIA: Do I?

72

DORA: As if you was waiting for something to 'appen.

OLIVIA: Oh?

DORA: Like an explosion. A bomb, or something.

OLIVIA (*smiling*): I don't think that's very likely. . . . (*Lowering her voice.*) Have you talked to Dan at all this week?

DORA: Never get the chance. 'E's too busy dancin' attendance on Madam Crocodile. . . .

> DAN *comes back from the bedroom, his cigarette-stub between his lips.*

(*Going towards the kitchen.*) I'm off. You don't catch me 'ere after dark.

DAN: Why, will ye be late for courting?

DORA: If I was, they'd wait for me. Good afternoon, Miss Grayne. Good afternoon . . . *sir*.

DAN (*winking at* OLIVIA): Are you sure they'd wait?

DORA: You ought to know.

> *She goes into the kitchen.* DAN *and* OLIVIA *are alone.*
> DAN *crosses to the sofa with a laugh, humming gaily.*

DAN: 'Their home addresses . . . and their caresses. . . .' (*He sits on the end of the sofa.*)

OLIVIA: You've been drinking, haven't you?

DAN (*after a pause, quizzically*): You don't miss much, do you?.

OLIVIA (*significantly*): No.

DAN (*rubbing his hands*): I've been drinking, and I feel fine! . . . (*Brandishing the Bible.*) You wouldn't like another dose of reading?

OLIVIA: I prefer talking.

DAN (*putting down the Bible*): Carry on.

OLIVIA: Asking questions.

DAN (*catching her eye*): Carry on! (*He studies his outspread hands.*)

73

OLIVIA (*crisply*): Are you sure you were ever a sailor! Are you sure you weren't a butcher?

> *A pause. He looks at her, slowly, then breaks the look abruptly.*

DAN (*rising with a smile and standing against the mantelpiece*): Aw, talkin's daft! *Doin's* the thing!

OLIVIA: You can talk too.

DAN: Aw, yes! D'you hear me just now? She's right, you know, I should ha' been a preacher. I remember, when I was a kid, sittin' in Sunday school – catching my mother's eye where she was sitting by the pulpit, with the sea behind her; and she pointed to the pulpit, and then to me, as if to say, that's the place for you. . . . (*Far away, pensive.*) I never forgot that.

> *A pause.*

OLIVIA: I don't believe a word of it.

DAN: Neither do I, but it sounds wonderful. (*Leaning over confidentially.*) I never saw my mam, and I never had a dad, and the first thing I remember is . . . Cardiff Docks. And you're the first 'oman I ever told that, so you can compliment yourself. Or the drink. (*Laughing.*) I think it's the drink.

OLIVIA: You *do* live in your imagination, don't you?

DAN (*reassuringly*): Yes. . . . It's the only way to bear with the awful things you have to do.

OLIVIA: What awful things?

DAN: Well. . . . (*Grinning like a child and going back to the sofa.*) Ah-ha! . . . I haven't had as much to drink as all that! (*Sitting on the sofa.*) Ah-ha! . . .

OLIVIA: You haven't a very high opinion of women, have you?

DAN *makes a gesture with his hands, pointing the thumbs downwards with a decisive movement.*

DAN: Women don't have to be drunk to talk.... You don't talk that much though, fair play. (*Looking her up and down, insolently.*) You're a dark horse, you are.

A pause. She rises abruptly and stands at the fireplace, her back to him. She takes off her spectacles.

Ye know, this isn't the life for you. What is there to it? Tell me that.

OLIVIA (*sombrely*): What is there to it ... ?

DAN: Yes. . . .

OLIVIA: Getting up at seven, mending my stockings or washing them, having breakfast with a vixenish old woman and spending the rest of the day with her, in a dreary house in the middle of a wood and going to bed at eleven. . . . I'm plain, I haven't got any money, I'm shy, and I haven't got any friends.

DAN (*teasing*): Don't you *like* the old lady?

OLIVIA: I could kill her. (*A pause. She realises what she has said.*)

DAN (*with a laugh*): Oh no, you couldn't! . . . Not many people have it in them to kill people. . . . Oh no!

She looks at him. A pause. He studies the palms of his hands, chuckling to himself.

OLIVIA: And what was there to *your* life at the Tallboys?

DAN: My life? Well. . . . The day don't start so good, with a lot of stuck-up boots to clean, and a lot of silly high heels all along the passage waitin' for a polish, and a lot of spoons to clean that's been in the mouths of gapin' fools that looks through me as if I was a dirty window hadn't been cleaned for years. . . . (*Throwing his stub into the fire in a sudden crescendo of fury.*) Orders, orders, orders;

75

go here, do this, don't do that you idiot, open the door
for me, get a move on – I was never meant to take orders,
never! . . . Down in the tea-place there's an old white
beard wigglin'. 'Waiter, my tea's stone cold.' (*Furiously.*)
I'm not a waiter, I'm a millionaire, and everybody's under
me! . . . And just when I think I got a bit o' peace . . .
(*his head in his hands*) . . . there's somebody . . . lockin' the
the bedroom door . . . (*raising his head*) . . . won't let me
get out; talk, talk, talk, won't fork out with no more
money, at me, at me, at me, won't put no clothes on,
calls me everythin', lie on the floor and screams and
screams, so nothin' keeps that mouth shut only . . .
(*A pause.*) It's raining out of the window, and the leaves
is off the trees . . . oh, Lord . . . I wish I could hear a bit
o' music . . . (*smiling, slowly*) . . . And I do, inside o' myself!
And I have a drop of drink . . . and everything's fine!
(*Excited.*) And when it's the night . . .

OLIVIA (*with a cry*): Go on!

    *A pause. He realises she is there, and turns slowly and
looks at her.*

DAN (*wagging his finger with a sly smile*): Aha! I'm too fly
for you! You'd like to know, wouldn't you? Aha! *Why*
would you like to know? (*Insistently, mischievously.*) Why
d'you lie awake . . . all night?

OLIVIA: Don't! . . . I'm frightened of you! . . .

DAN (*triumphantly, rising and facing her, his back half to
the audience*): Why?

OLIVIA (*desperate*): How do you know I lie awake at
night? Shall I tell you why? Because you're awake yourself. You *can't sleep!* There's one thing that keeps you
awake . . . isn't there? One thing you've pushed into the
back of your mind and you can't do any more about it,

and you never will. . . . And do you know what it is ? . . .
It's a little thing. A box. Only a box. But it's . . . rather
heavy. . . .

> DAN *looks at her. A long pause. He jerks away with a*
> *laugh and sits at the sofa again.*

DAN (*quietly, prosaically*): The way you was going
through my letters the other day – that had to make me
smile. . . .

> *His voice dies away. Without warning, as if seeing*
> *something in his mind which makes him lose control, he*
> *shrieks loudly, clapping his hands over his eyes: then is*
> *silent. He recovers slowly and stares at her. After a*
> *pause, in a measured voice.*

It's the only thing that keeps me awake, mind you! The
only thing! (*Earnestly.*) But I don't know what to do. . . .
You see, nothing worries me, nothing in the world, only
. . . I don't like a pair of eyes staring at me . . . (*his voice*
trailing away) . . . with no look in them. I don't know what
to do . . . I don't know. . . .

> *Without warning he bursts into tears. She sits beside*
> *him and seems almost about to put her arms about him.*
> *He feels she is there, looks into her eyes, grasps her arm,*
> *then pulls himself together, abruptly.*

(*Rising.*) But it's the only thing! I live by myself . . .
(*slapping his chest*) . . . inside here – and all the rest of you
can go to hang. *After* I've made a use of you, though!
Nothing's going to stop me! I feel fine! I——

> BELSIZE *crosses outside. A sharp knock at the front*
> *door. She half rises. He motions her to sit again.*

(*With his old swagger.*) All right! Anybody's there, I'll
deal with 'em—— I'll manage myself all right! You watch
me! (*He goes to the front door and opens it.*)

BELSIZE (*at the door, jovially*): Hello Dan! How's things ?

DAN (*letting him in and shutting the door*): Not so bad. . . .
(*He brings* BELSIZE *into the room.*)

BELSIZE (*as* OLIVIA *goes*): Afternoon, Miss Grayne!

OLIVIA (*putting on her spectacles*): How do you do . . . .
(*She makes an effort to compose herself and hurries across to the sun-room.*)

BELSIZE'S *attitude is one of slightly exaggerated breeziness:* DAN'S *is one of cheerful naïveté almost as limpid as on his first appearance.*

BELSIZE: Bearing up, eh?

DAN: Yes, sir, bearin' up, you know. . . .

BELSIZE: We haven't scared you all out of the house, yet, I see!

DAN: No chance!

BELSIZE: All these blood-curdlers, eh?

DAN: I should say so!

BELSIZE: No more news for me, I suppose?

DAN: No chance!

BELSIZE: Ah . . . too bad. Mind if I sit down?

DAN (*pointing to the sofa*): Well, this is the nearest you get to comfort in this house, sir.

BELSIZE: No, thanks, this'll do. . . . (*Sitting on a chair at the table, and indicating the cuttings.*) I see you keep apace of the news.

DAN: I should say so! They can't hardly wait for the latest on the case in this house, sir.

BELSIZE: Ah, well, it's only natural . . . I got a bit of a funny feeling bottom of my spine myself crossing by the rubbish heap.

DAN: Well, will you have a cigarette, sir? . . . (*His hand to his jacket pocket.*) Only a Woodbine——

BELSIZE: No, thanks.

78

DAN (*after a pause*): Would you like to see Mrs Bramson, sir?

BELSIZE: Oh, plenty of time. How's she bearing up?

DAN: Well, it's been a bit of a shock for her, them finding the remains of the lady at the bottom of her garden, you know.

BELSIZE: The remains of the lady! I wish you wouldn't talk like that. I've seen 'em.

DAN (*looking over his shoulder at the cuttings*): Well, you see, I haven't.

BELSIZE: You know, I don't mind telling you, they reckon the fellow that did this job was a bloodstained clever chap.

DAN (*smiling*): You don't say?

BELSIZE (*casually*): He was blackmailing her, you know.

DAN: Tch! tch! Was he?

BELSIZE: Whoever he was.

DAN: She had a lot of fellows on a string, though, didn't she?

BELSIZE (*guardedly*): That's true.

DAN: Though this one seems to have made a bit more stir than any of the others, don't he?

BELSIZE: Yes. (*Indicating the cuttings.*) Regular film star. Made his name.

DAN (*abstractedly*): If you *can* make your name without nobody knowin' what it is, o' course.

BELSIZE (*slightly piqued*): Yes, of course. . . . But I don't reckon he's been as bright as all that.

DAN (*after a pause*): Oh, you don't?

BELSIZE: No! They'll nab him in no time.

DAN: Oh . . . Mrs Bramson'll be that relieved. And the whole country besides. . . .

BELSIZE: Look here, Dan, any self-respecting murderer

would have taken care to mutilate the body to such a
degree that nobody could recognise it – and here we come
and identify it first go!

> DAN *folds his arms and looks thoughtful.*

Call that clever? . . . What d'you think?

> DAN *catches his eye and crosses to the sofa.*

DAN: Well sir, I'm a slow thinker, I am, but though it
might be clever to leave the lady unide – unide——

BELSIZE: Unidentified.

DAN (*sitting on the edge of the sofa*): Thank you, sir. . . .
(*Laboriously.*) Well, though it be clever to leave the lady
unidentified and not be caught . . . hasn't he been more
clever to leave her identified . . . and still not be caught?

BELSIZE: Why didn't you sleep in your bed on the night
of the tenth?

> *A pause.* DAN *stiffens almost imperceptibly.*

DAN: What you say?

BELSIZE: Why didn't you sleep in your bed on the night
of the murder?

DAN: I did.

BELSIZE (*lighting his pipe*): You didn't.

DAN: Yes, I did. Oh – except for about half an hour –
that's right. I couldn't sleep for toffee and I went up the
fire-escape – I remember thinkin' about it next day when
the woman was missing, and trying to remember if I
could think of anything funny——

BELSIZE: What time was that? (*He rises, crosses to the
fireplace, and throws his match into it.*)

DAN: Oh, about . . . oh, you know how you wake up
in the night and don't know what time it is. . . .

BELSIZE (*staring at him doubtfully*): Mmm. . . .

DAN: I could never sleep when I was at sea, neither,
sir.

BELSIZE: Mmm. (*Suddenly.*) Are you feeling hot?

DAN: No.

BELSIZE: Your shirt's wet through.

DAN (*after a pause*): I've been sawin' some wood.

BELSIZE: Why didn't you tell us you were having an affair with the deceased woman?

DAN: Affair? What's that?

BELSIZE: Come along, old chap, I'll use a straighter word if it'll help you. But you're stalling. She was seen by two of the maids talking to you in the shrubbery. Well?

> *A pause.* DAN *bursts into tears, but with a difference. His breakdown a few minutes ago was genuine; this is a good performance, very slightly exaggerated.* BELSIZE *watches him dispassionately, his brows knit.*

DAN: Oh, sir . . . it's been on my conscience . . . ever since. . . .

BELSIZE: So you did have an affair with her?

DAN: Oh no, sir, not that! I avoided her ever after that day she stopped me, sir! . . . You see, sir, a lady stayin' where I was workin', an' for all I knew married, an' all the other fellers she'd been after, and the brazen way she went on to me. . . . You're only human, aren't you, sir, and when they asked me about her, I got frightened to tell about her stopping me. . . . But now you know about it, sir, it's a weight off my mind, you wouldn't believe. . . . (*Rising, after seeming to pull himself together.*) As a matter of fact, it was the disgust-like of nearly gettin' mixed up with her that was keepin' me awake at nights.

BELSIZE: I see. . . . You're a bit of a milk-sop, aren't you?

DAN (*apparently puzzled*): Am I, sir?

BELSIZE: Yes. . . . That'll be all for today. I'll let you
off this once.

DAN: I'm that relieved, sir!

BELSIZE (*crossing to the table for his hat*): But don't try
and keep things from the police another time.

DAN: No chance!

BELSIZE: They always find out, you know.

DAN: Yes, sir. Would you like a cup o' tea, sir?

BELSIZE: No, thanks. I've got another inquiry in the
village. . . . (*Turning back, with an after thought.*) Oh, just
one thing – might as well just do it, we're supposed to
with all the chaps we're questioning, matter of form – if
you don't mind, I'll have a quick look through your
luggage. Matter of form. . . .

DAN: Oh yes.

BELSIZE: Where d'you hang out?

DAN (*tonelessly*): Through the kitchen . . . here, sir. . . .
First door facin'. . . .

BELSIZE: First door, facing——

DAN: You can't miss it.

BELSIZE: I'll find it.

DAN: It's open, I think.

> BELSIZE *goes into the kitchen. A pause.* DAN *looks
> slowly round the room.*

(*Turning mechanically to the kitchen door.*) You can't miss
it. . . .

> *A pause. The noise of something being moved, beyond the
> kitchen.* DAN *sits on the sofa with a jerk, looking before
> him. His fingers beat a rapid tattoo on the sides of the sofa.
> He looks at them, rises convulsively and walks round the
> room, grasping chairs and furniture as he goes. He
> returns to the sofa, sits, and begins the tattoo again. With
> a sudden wild automatic movement he beats his closed fists*

in rapid succession against the sides of his head. BELSIZE
returns carrying the hat-box.

BELSIZE (*crossing and placing the hat-box on the table*): This
one's locked. Have you got the key?

DAN *rises, and takes a step into the middle of the room.*
He looks at the hat-box at last.

DAN (*in a dead voice*): It isn't mine.

BELSIZE: Not yours?

DAN: No.

BELSIZE: Oh? . . . Whose is it, then?

DAN: I dunno. It isn't mine.

OLIVIA *stands at the sun-room door.*

OLIVIA: I'm sorry, I thought . . . Why, Inspector, what
are you doing with my box?

BELSIZE: Yours?

OLIVIA: It's got all my letters in it!

BELSIZE: But it was in . . .

OLIVIA: Oh, Dan's room used to be the box-
room.

BELSIZE: Oh, I see. . . .

OLIVIA: I'll keep it in my wardrobe; it'll be safer
there. . . .

With sudden feverish resolution, she picks up the box
and carries it into the kitchen. DAN *looks the other way as*
she passes him.

BELSIZE: I'm very sorry, miss. (*Scratching his head.*) I'm
afraid I've offended her. . . .

DAN (*smiling*): She'll be all right, sir. . . .

BELSIZE: Well, young feller, I'll be off. You might tell
the old lady I popped in, and hope she's better.

DAN (*smiling and nodding*): Thank you, sir. . . . Good
day, sir.

BELSIZE: Good day.

He goes out through the front door into the twilight, closing it behind him.

DAN: Good day, sir. . . .

A pause. DAN *crumples to the floor in a dead faint.*

QUICK CURTAIN

ACT III

SCENE I

Half an hour later. The light has waned; the fire is lit and throws a red reflection into the room. DAN *is lying on the sofa, eyes closed.* NURSE LIBBY *sits at the end of the sofa holding his pulse.* MRS TERENCE *stands behind the sofa with a toby jug of water.*

NURSE: There, lovey, you won't be long now. . . . Ever so much steadier already. . . . What a bit o' luck me blowin' in today! . . . Tt! tt! Pouring with sweat, the lad is. Whatever's he been up to?

MRS TERENCE: When I walked in that door and saw 'im lyin' full stretch on that floor everything went topsy-wopsy. (*Pressing the jug to* DAN's *lips.*) It did! The room went round and round. . . .

NURSE (*as* DAN *splutters*): Don't choke 'im, there's a love. . . .

MRS TERENCE: D'you know what I said to meself when I saw 'im lyin' there?

NURSE: What?

MRS TERENCE: I said, 'That murderer's been at 'im,' I said, 'and it's the next victim.' I did!

NURSE: So you would! Just like the pictures. . . . 'Old your 'ead up, love. . . .

MRS TERENCE (*as* NURSE LIBBY *supports* DAN's *head*): Got a *nice* face, 'asn't he?

NURSE: Oh *yes*! . . . (*As* DAN's *eyes flicker.*) Shh, he's

85

coming to. . . . (DAN *opens his eyes and looks at her*.) Welcome back to the land of the living!

MRS TERENCE: Thought the murderer'd got you!

A pause. DAN *stares, then sits up abruptly.*

DAN: How long I been like that?

NURSE: We picked you up ten minutes ago, and I'd say it was twenty minutes before that, roughly-like, that you passed away.

MRS TERENCE: Passed away, don't frighten the boy! . . . Whatever come over you, dear!

DAN: I dunno. Felt sick, I think. (*Recovering himself.*) Say no more about it, eh? Don't like swinging the lead. . . . (*His head in his hand.*)

MRS TERENCE: Waiting 'and and foot on Madam Crocodile, enough to wear King Kong out. . . .

NURSE: That's better, eh?

DAN: It is really getting dark?

MRS TERENCE: It's a scandal the way the days are drawin' in. . . . 'Ave another sip——

DAN (*as she makes to give him more water, to* NURSE LIBBY): You haven't such a thing as a nip of brandy?

NURSE (*opening her bag*): Yes, lovey, I nearly gave you a drop just now——

DAN *takes a flask from her and gulps; he takes a second mouthful. He gives it back, shakes himself, and looks before him.*

MRS TERENCE: Better?

DAN: Yes. . . . Clears the brain no end. . . . Makes you understand better. . . . (*His voice growing in vehemence.*) Makes you see what a damn silly thing it is to get the wind up about anything. *Do* things! Get a move on! Show 'em what you're made of! Get a move on! . . . Fainting indeed. . . . Proper girl's trick, I'm ashamed o' meself. . . . (*Looking round, quietly.*) The light's going . . . the daytime's as if it's never been; it's dead. . . . (*Seeing the others stare, with a laugh.*) Daft, isn't it?

> DORA *brings in an oil lamp from the kitchen; she is wearing her outdoor clothes. She crosses to the table, strikes a match with her back to the audience and lights the lamp, then the wall light. The twilight is dispelled.*

NURSE (*shutting her bag, rising*): You'll be all right; a bit light-headed after the fall I expect. (*Going to the hall.*) Well, got an abscess the other side of Turneyfield, *and* a slow puncture. So long, lovey.

DAN (*sitting up*): So long!

NURSE: Be good, all!

> *She bustles out of the front door. A pause.* DAN *sits looking before him, drumming his fingers on the sofa.*

DORA (*closing the right window-curtains*): What's the matter with him?

MRS TERENCE: Conked out.

DORA: Conked out? Oh, dear. . . . D'you think 'e see'd something? I'll tell you what it is!

MRS TERENCE (*closing the left window-curtains*): What?

DORA: The monster's lurking again.

> *Mechanically* DAN *takes a box of matches and a cigarette from his pocket.*

MRS TERENCE: I'll give you lurk, my girl, look at the egg on my toby! Why don't you learn to wash up, instead of walkin' about talking like three-halfpennyworth of trash?

DORA: I can't wash up properly in that kitchen; with that light. Them little oil lamps isn't any good except to set the place on fire. (*She goes into the kitchen.*)

> DAN *drums his fingers on the sofa.* MRS BRAMSON *wheels herself from the bedroom.*

MRS BRAMSON: I dropped off. Why didn't somebody wake me? Have I been missing something?

MRS TERENCE: That Inspector Belsize called.

MRS BRAMSON (*testily*): Then why didn't somebody wake me? Dan, what did he want?

DAN: Just a friendly call.

MRS BRAMSON: You seem very far away, dear. What's the matter with you? . . . Dan!

DAN: Bit of an 'eadache, that's all.

MRS BRAMSON: Doesn't make you deaf, though, dear, does it?

MRS TERENCE: Now, now, turnin' against the apple of your eye; can't 'ave that goin' on——

  A sharp knock at the front door. DAN *starts up and goes towards the hall.*

MRS BRAMSON (*to* MRS TERENCE): See who it is.

MRS TERENCE (*at the front door, as* DAN *is about to push past her*): Oh . . . it's only the paraffin boy. . . . (*To the boy outside, taking a can from him.*) And you bring stuff on a Saturday night another time.

  DAN *is standing behind* MRS BRAMSON'S *chair.*

MRS BRAMSON: I should think so——

  MRS TERENCE *comes into the room.* DAN *strikes a match for his cigarette.*

MRS TERENCE (*with a cry*): Oh! Can't you see this is paraffin? (*She puts the can on the floor just outside the hall.*)

MRS BRAMSON: You went through my side like a knife——

MRS TERENCE: If people knew what to do with their money, they'd put electric light in their 'omes 'stead of dangerin' people's lives.

  She goes into the kitchen. DAN *stares before him, the match flickering.*

MRS BRAMSON (*blowing out the match*): You'll burn your fingers! Set yourself on fire! Absent-minded! . . . I woke up all of a cold shiver. Had a terrible dream.

DAN (*mechanically*): What about?

MRS BRAMSON: Horrors . . . I'm freezing. Get me my shawl off my bed, will you, dear? . . . (*As he does not move.*) My shawl, dear!

>   DAN *starts, collects himself, and smiles his most ingratiating smile.*

DAN: I *am* sorry, mum. In the Land of Nod, I was! Let me see, what was it your highness was after? A shawl? No sooner said than done. . . . You watch me! One, two, three! (*He runs into the bedroom.*)

MRS BRAMSON: Silly boy . . . silly boy. . . .

>   OLIVIA *comes in quickly from the kitchen. She is dressed to go out and carries a suitcase.*

Where are you off to?

OLIVIA: I've had a telegram. A friend of mine in London's very ill.

MRS BRAMSON: What's the matter with her?

OLIVIA: Pneumonia.

MRS BRAMSON: Where's the telegram?

OLIVIA: I – I threw it away.

MRS BRAMSON: Where d'you throw it?

OLIVIA: I – I threw it away.

MRS BRAMSON: You haven't had any telegram.

OLIVIA (*impatiently*): No, I haven't!

MRS BRAMSON: What's the matter with you?

OLIVIA: I can't stay in this house tonight.

MRS BRAMSON: Why not?

OLIVIA: I'm frightened.

MRS BRAMSON: Oh, don't be——

OLIVIA: Listen to me. I've never known before what

it was to be terrified. But when I saw today beginning to end, and tonight getting nearer and nearer . . . I felt my finger-tips getting cold. And I knew it was fright . . . stark fright. I'm not a fool, and I'm not hysterical . . . but I've been sitting in my room looking at myself in the glass, trying to control myself, telling myself what are real things . . . and what aren't. I don't know any longer. The day's over. The forest's all round us. Anything may happen. . . . You shouldn't stay in this house tonight. That's all.

MRS BRAMSON (*blustering*): It's very silly of you, trying to scare an old woman with a weak heart. What have you to be frightened of?

OLIVIA: There's been a murder, you know.

MRS BRAMSON: Nobody's going to murder *you*! Besides, we've got Danny to look after us. He's as strong as an ox, and no silly nerves about him . . . what *is* it you're afraid of?

OLIVIA: I——

MRS BRAMSON: Shy, aren't you? . . . Where are you staying tonight?

OLIVIA: In Langbury, with Hubert Laurie and his sister.

MRS BRAMSON: Not too frightened to make arrangements with *him*, eh.

OLIVIA: Arrangements?

MRS BRAMSON: Well, some people would call it something else.

OLIVIA (*losing her temper*): Oh, won't you see. . . .

MRS BRAMSON: I'm very annoyed with you. How are you going to get there?

OLIVIA: Walking.

MRS BRAMSON: Through the forest? Not too frightened for that, I see.

OLIVIA: I'd rather spend tonight in the forest than in this house.

MRS BRAMSON: That sounds convincing, I must say. Well, you can go, but when you come back, I'm not so sure I shall answer the door. Think that over in the morning.

OLIVIA: The morning? . . .

DAN'S VOICE (*in the bedroom, singing*): '. . . their home addresses . . . and their caresses . . . linger in my memory of those beautiful dames. . . .'

> OLIVIA *listens, holding her breath; she tries to say something to* MRS BRAMSON, *and fails. She makes an effort, and runs out of the front door. It bangs behind her.* DAN *comes back from the bedroom, carrying the shawl.*

DAN (*over-casual*): What was that at the door?

MRS BRAMSON: My niece. Gone for the night, if you please.

DAN: Gone . . . for the night? (*He stares before him.*)

MRS BRAMSON: Would you believe it? Says she's frightened. . . . (*A pause.*) Come along with the shawl, dear, I'm freezing. . . .

DAN (*with a laugh, putting the shawl round her*): Don't know what's up with me——

> *He goes to the table and looks at a newspaper.* MRS TERENCE *comes in from the kitchen, her coat on.*

MRS TERENCE: Well, I must go on my way rejoicin'.

MRS BRAMSON: Everybody seems to be going. What *is* all this?

MRS TERENCE: What d'you want for lunch tomorrow?

MRS BRAMSON: Lunch tomorrow? . . . Let me see. . . .

DAN: Lunch? Tomorrow? . . . (*After a pause.*) What about a nice little steak?

MRS BRAMSON: A steak, let me see. . . . Yes, with baked potatoes——

DAN: And a nice roly-poly puddin', the kind you like?

MRS BRAMSON: I think so.

MRS TERENCE: Something light. O.K. Good night.

    She goes back into the kitchen. DAN *scans the newspaper casually.*

MRS BRAMSON (*inquisitive*): What are you reading, dear?

DAN (*breezily*): Only the murder again. About the clues that wasn't any good.

MRS BRAMSON (*suddenly*): Danny, *d'you* think Olivia's a thief?

DAN: Shouldn't be surprised.

MRS BRAMSON: What!

DAN: Her eyes wasn't very wide apart.

MRS BRAMSON (*working herself up*): Goodness me . . . my jewel-box . . . what a fool I was to let her go – my ear-rings . . . the double-faced——

    She wheels herself furiously into her bedroom. DORA, *her hat and coat on, comes in from the kitchen in time to see her go.*

DORA: What's up with her?

DAN (*still at his paper*): Think's she been robbed.

DORA: Oh, is that all. . . . That's the fourth time this month she's thought that. One of these days something *will* 'appen to her and will I be pleased? Oh, baby! . . . Where's Mrs Terence?

DAN: Gone, I think.

DORA (*frightened*): Oh, law, no! (*Calling.*) Mrs Terence!

MRS TERENCE (*calling in the kitchen*): Ye'es!

DORA: You 'aven't gone without me, 'ave you?

MRS TERENCE (*appearing at the kitchen door, spearing a hatpin into her hat.*) Yes, I'm 'alf-way there, what d'you think?

DORA: You did give me a turn! (*Going to the table and taking the box.*) I think I'll 'ave a choc. (*Walking towards the hall.*) I couldn't 'ave walked a step in those trees all by myself. Coming?

DAN (*suddenly*): I'd have come with you with pleasure, only I'm going the other direction. Payley Hill way.

MRS TERENCE (*surprised*): *You* going out?

DORA: Oh?

DAN (*in the hall, putting on hat and mackintosh*): Yes, I still feel a bit funny.

MRS TERENCE: But you can't leave 'er 'ere by herself!

DORA: She'll scream the place down!

DAN (*over-explanatory*): I asked her, this very minute, and she don't seem to mind. You know what she is. Said it'll do me good, and won't hear of my stayin'. It's no good arguin' with her.

DORA *puts the chocolates down on the occasional table. She and* MRS TERENCE *follow* DAN *into the hall.*

DORA: No good arguin' with her – don't I know it!

MRS TERENCE: You 'ave a nice walk while you get the chance; you wait on 'er too much. . . . (*Closing the plush curtains so that they are all out of sight.*) Ooh, ain't it dark. . . . Got the torch, Dora?

DORA: O.K., honey.

MRS TERENCE: Laws, I'd be frightened goin' off by meself. . . . Well, we'd best 'urry, Dora. . . . Good night, Dan. Pity you aren't coming our way——

DAN'S VOICE: See you in the morning! Good night!

DORA'S VOICE: O.K.! . . . Toodle-oo!

The door bangs. A pause.

DAN'S VOICE (*outside the left window*): Good night!

MRS TERENCE'S VOICE (*outside the right window*): Good night!

DORA (*same*): Good night!
> *Silence.*

MRS TERENCE (*farther away*): Good night!

DORA (*same*): Good night!
> MRS BRAMSON *comes trundling back from the bedroom in her chair.*

MRS BRANSOM: Good night here, good night there; anybody'd think it was the night before Judgement Day. What's the matter with ... (*Seeing the room is empty.*) Talking to myself. Wish people wouldn't walk out of rooms and leave me high and dry. Don't like it. (*She wheels herself round to the table. A pause. She looks round impatiently.*) Where's my chocolates? ...
> *She looks round again, gets up out of her chair for the first time in the play, walks quite normally across the room to the mantelpiece, sees her chocolates are not there, walks up to the occasional table, and takes up the box.*

That girl's been at them again ...
> *She walks back to her chair, carrying the chocolates, and sits in it again. She begins to munch. She suddenly stops, as if she has heard something.*

What's that? ...
> *She listens again. A cry is heard far away.*

Oh, God ... Danny!
> *The cry is repeated.*

Danny!
> *The cry is heard a third time.*

It's an owl ... Oh, Lord!
> *She falls back in relief, and eats another chocolate.*

94

*The clock strikes the half-hour. Silence. The silence gets
on her nerves.*

(*After a pause, calling softly.*) Danny! ... (*As there is no
answer.*) What's the boy doing in that kitchen?

*She takes up the newspaper, sees a headline, and puts
it down hastily. She sees the Bible on the table, opens it,
and turns over pages.*

(*After a pause, suddenly.*) I've got the jitters. I've got the
jitters. I've got the jitters. ... (*Calling loudly.*) Danny!

*She waits; there is complete silence. She rises, walks
over to the kitchen door, and flings it wide open.*

(*Shouting.*) Danny! (*No reply.*) He's gone. ... They've
all gone. ... They've left me. ... (*Losing control, beating
her hands wildly on her Bible.*) Oh, Lord, help a poor
woman. ... They've left me! (*Tottering to the sun-room.*)
Danny ... where are you? ... Danny. ... I'm going to
be murdered. ... I'm going to be murdered! ... Danny. ...
(*Her voice rising, until she is shrieking hysterically.*) Danny!
Danny! Danny!

*She stops suddenly. Footsteps on the gravel outside
the front door.*

(*In a strangled whisper.*) There's something outside ...
something outside. ... Oh, heavens. ... (*Staggering
across to the sofa.*) Danny, where are you? Where are
you? There's something outs—

*The front door bangs. She collapses on the sofa,
terrified, her enormous Bible clasped to her breast.*

Oh, Lord, help me ... help me. ... Oh, Lord, help ...
(*Muttering, her eyes closed.*) ... Forgive us our trespasses ...

The curtains are suddenly parted. It is DAN, *a cigarette
between his lips. He stands motionless, his feet planted
apart, holding the curtains. There is murder in his face.
She is afraid to look, but is forced to at last.*

95

Danny . . . Oh . . . Oh . . .

DAN (*smiling, suddenly normal and reassuring*): That's all right. . . . It's only Danny. . . .

MRS BRAMSON: Thank God. . . . (*Going off into laughing hysteria.*) Ah . . . ah . . . ah. . . .

> DAN *throws his cigarette away, lays his hat on the occasional table, throws his mackintosh on the left window-seat, and sits beside her, patting her, looking round to see no one has heard her cries.*

I'll never forgive you, never. Oh, my heart. . . . Oh, oh – oh——

> *He runs across to the medicine cupboard and brings back a brandy bottle and two glasses.*

DAN: Now have a drop of this. . . . (*As she winces at the taste.*) Go on, do you good. . . . (*As she drinks.*) I am sorry, I am really. . . . You see, they wanted me to see them to the main path, past the rubbish-heap, see, in case they were frightened. . . . Now, that's better, isn't it?

> *They are seated side by side on the sofa.*

MRS BRAMSON: I don't know yet. . . . Give me some more. . . . (*He pours one out for her, and one for himself. They drink.*) All alone, I was. . . . (*Her face puckering with self pity.*) Just an old woman calling for help . . . (*her voice breaking*) . . . and no answer.

DAN (*putting the bottle on the floor beside him*): Poor old mum, runnin' about lookin' for Danny——

MRS BRAMSON (*sharply*): I wasn't running about as much as all that. . . . Oh, the relief when I saw your face——

DAN: I bet you wasn't half glad, eh?

MRS BRAMSON: You're the only one that understands me, Danny, that's what you are——

DAN (*patting her*): That's right——

MRS BRAMSON: I don't have to tell you everything I've been through. I don't have to tell you about my husband, how unkind and ungodly he was – I wouldn't have minded so much him being ungodly, but oh, he *was* unkind. . . . (*Sipping.*) And I don't have to tell *you* how unkind he was. You know. You just know . . . whatever else I've not been, I was *always* a great one on psychology.

DAN: You was. (*He takes her glass and fills it again, and his own.*)

MRS BRAMSON: I'm glad those other people have gone. Awful screeching common women. Answer back, answer back, answer back. . . . Isn't it time for my medicine? (*He hands her glass back. They both drink. He sits smiling and nodding at her.*) That day you said to me about me reminding you of your mother. . . . (*As he slowly begins to roll up his sleeves a little way.*) These poets and rubbishy people can think all they like about their verses and sonnets and such – that girl Olivia writes sonnets – would you believe it——

DAN: Fancy.

MRS BRAMSON: They can think all they like, that was a beautiful thought. (*Her arm on his shoulder.*) And when you think you're just an ignorant boy, it's . . . it's startling.

DAN (*with a laugh*): That's right.

MRS BRAMSON: I'll never forget that. Not as long as I live. . . . (*Trying to stem the tears.*) I want a chocolate now.

DAN: Right you are! . . . (*Placing her glass and his own on the floor and walking briskly to the table.*) A nice one with a soft centre, the kind you like. . . . Why, here's one straight away. . . . (*He walks slowly to the back of the sofa.*) *In a level voice.*) Now shut your eyes . . . open you mouth. . . .

MRS BRAMSON (*purring*): Oh, Danny. . . . You're the only one. . . .

> *She shuts her eyes. He stands behind her, and puts the chocolate into her mouth. His fingers close slowly and involuntarily, over her neck; she feels his touch, and draws both his hands down, giggling, so that his face almost touches hers.*

(*Maudlin.*) What strong hands they are. . . . You're a pet, my little chubby-face, my baby-face, my Danny. . . . Am I in a draught? (*A pause.* DAN *draws his hands slowly away, walks to the back, and shuts the plush curtains.*) I've got to take care of myself, haven't I?

DAN (*turning slowly and looking at her*): You have.

> *He picks up the paraffin can briskly and goes towards the kitchen.*

MRS BRAMSON: What are you——

DAN: Only takin' the paraffin tin in the kitchen.

> *He goes into the kitchen.*

MRS BRAMSON (*half to herself*): That girl should have carried it in. Anything to annoy me. Tomorrow—— (*Turning and seeing that he is gone.*) Danny! (*Shrieking suddenly.*) Danny!

> DAN *runs back from the kitchen.*

DAN: What's the matter?

> *He looks hastily towards the hall to see no one has heard.*

MRS BRAMSON: Oh dear, I thought——

DAN (*sitting on the back of the sofa*): I was only putting the paraffin away. Now—— (*He leans over the sofa, and raises his arms slowly.*)

MRS BRAMSON (*putting her hand on his arm*): I think I'll go to bed now.

DAN (*after a pause, dropping his arm*): O.K.

MRS BRAMSON: And I'll have my supper-tray in my

room. (*Petulantly.*) Get me back into my chair, dear, will you?

DAN (*jerkily*): O.K. (*He crosses to the invalid chair.*)

MRS BRAMSON: Has she put the glass by the bed for my teeth?

DAN (*bringing over the chair*): I put it there myself. (*He helps her into the chair and pulls it over towards the bedroom.*)

MRS BRAMSON (*suddenly, in the middle of the room*): I want to be read to now.

DAN (*after a pause of indecision*): O.K. (*Clapping his hands, effusively.*) What'll you have? The old *East Lynne*?

MRS BRAMSON: No. I don't feel like anything sentimental tonight. . . .

DAN (*looking towards the desk*): What'll you have then?

MRS BRAMSON: I think I'd like the Bible.

A pause. He looks at her.

DAN: O.K.

MRS BRAMSON (*as he goes smartly to the sofa, fetches the Bible, pulls up a chair to the right of her, sits and looks for the place*): That piece you were reading. . . . It's Sunday . . . . Isn't that nice . . . all the aches and pains quiet for once . . . pretty peaceful. . . .

DAN (*reading*): 'Blessed is the man that walketh not in the counsel of the ungodly, nor standeth in the way of sinners, nor sitteth in the seat of the scornful. . . .'

MRS BRAMSON (*drowsily*): You read so nicely, Danny.

DAN: Very kind of you, my lady. (*Reading a little breathlessly.*) 'But his delight is in the law of the Lord; and in His law doth he meditate day and night——'

MRS BRAMSON: Sh!

DAN: What? Can you hear something?

MRS BRAMSON: Yes! A sort of – thumping noise. . . . (*She looks at him suddenly, leans forward, and puts her right hand inside his jacket.*) Why, Danny, it's you! It's your heart . . . beating! (*He laughs.*) Are you all right dear?

DAN: Fine. I been running along the path, see. . . . (*Garrulously.*) I been out of training, I suppose; when I was at sea I never missed a day running round the decks, o' course. . . .

MRS BRAMSON (*sleepily*): Of course. . . .

DAN (*speaking quickly, as if eager to conjure up a vision*): I remember those mornings – on some sea – very misty – pale it is, with the sun like breathing silver where he's coming' up across the water, but not blowin' on the sea at all . . . and the sea-gulls standing on the deck-rail looking at themselves in the water on the deck, and only me about and nothing else. . . .

MRS BRAMSON (*nodding sleepily*): Yes. . . .

DAN: And the sun. Just me and the sun.

MRS BRAMSON (*nodding*): There's no sun now, dear; it's night!

   .A pause. He drums his fingers on the Bible.

DAN: Yes . . . it's night now. (*Reading, feverishly.*) 'The ungodly are not so, but are like the chaff which the wind driveth away——'

MRS BRAMSON: I think I'll go to bye-byes. . . . We'll have the rest tomorrow, shall we? (*Testily.*) Help me, dear, help me, you know what I am——

DAN (*drumming his fingers: suddenly, urgently*): Wait a minute. . . . I – I've only got two more verses——

MRS BRAMSON: Hurry it up, dear. I don't want to wake up in the morning with a nasty cold.

DAN (*reading slowly*): '. . . Therefore the ungodly shall not stand in the judgment, nor sinners in the congregation of the righteous. . . . For the Lord knoweth the way of the righteous . . . but the way of the ungodly . . . shall perish. . . .'

> *A pause. He shuts the Bible loudly, and lays it on the table.* MRS BRAMSON *can hardly keep awake.*

That's the end.

MRS BRAMSON: Is it? . . . Ah, well, it's been a long day——

DAN: Are you quite comfortable?

MRS BRAMSON: A bit achy. Glad to go to bed. Hope that woman's put my bottle in all right. Bet she hasn't——

DAN: Sure you're comfortable? Wouldn't you like a cushion back of your head?

MRS BRAMSON: No dear, just wheel me——

DAN (*rising*): I think you'll be more comfortable with a cushion. (*Rising, humming.*) 'I'm a pretty little feller, everybody knows . . . dunno what to call me . . .'

> *He goes deliberately across, humming, and picks up a large black cushion from the sofa. His hands close on the cushion and he stands silent a moment. He moves slowly back to the other side of her; he stands looking at her, his back three-quarters to the audience and his face hidden: he is holding the cushion in both hands.*

> MRS BRAMSON *shakes herself out of sleep and looks at him.*

MRS BRAMSON: What a funny look on your face, dear. Smiling like that. . . . (*Foolishly.*) You look so kind. . . .

> *He begins to raise the cushion slowly.*

So kind. . . . (*Absently.*) What are you going to do with that cushion? . . .

> *The lights dim gradually into complete darkness, and the music grows into a thunderous crescendo.*

SCENE II

*The music plays a few bars, then dies down proportionately as
    the lights come up again.*

    *Half an hour later. The scene is the same, with the same
    lighting; the room is empty and the wheel-chair has been
    removed.*

    DAN *comes in from the sun-room, smoking the stub of
    a cigarette. He crosses smartly, takes the bottle and glasses
    from the floor by the sofa and places them on the table, pours
    himself a quick drink, places the bottle on the floor next
    the desk, throws away his stub, takes another cigarette
    from his pocket, puts it in his mouth, takes out a box of
    matches, and lights a match. The clock chimes. He looks
    at it, seems to make a decision, blows out the match, throws
    the matchbox on the table, takes Mrs Bramson's tape and
    keys from his trouser pocket, crosses quietly to the safe by
    the fireplace, opens it, takes out the cash-box, sits on the
    sofa, unlocks the cash-box, stuffs the keys back into his
    trousers, opens the cash-box, takes out the notes, looks at
    them, delighted, stuffs them into his pockets, hurries into the
    sun-room, returns a second later with the empty invalid chair,
    plants it in the middle of the room, picks up the cushion from
    the floor above the table, looks at it a moment, arrested,
    throws it callously on the invalid chair, hurries into the kit-
    chen, returns immediately with the paraffin, sprinkles it free-
    ly over the invalid chair, places the can under the table, lifts
    the paraffin lamp from the table, and is just about to smash it
    over the invalid chair when there is a sound of a chair falling
    over in the sun-room. His face inscrutable, he looks towards
    it. He carries the lamp stealthily to the desk, puts it down,
    looks round, picks a chair from near the table, and stands
    at the sun-room door with the chair held high above his head.*

The stagger of footsteps; OLIVIA *stands in the door-*
way to the sun-room. She has been running through the
forest; her clothes are wild, her hair has fallen about her
shoulders, and she is no longer wearing spectacles. She looks
nearly beautiful. Her manner is quiet, almost dazed. DAN
lowers the chair slowly and sits on the other side of the table.
A pause.

OLIVIA: I've never seen a dead body before . . . I
climbed through the window and nearly fell over it. Like
a sack of potatoes or something. I thought it was, at
first. . . . And that's murder. (*As he looks up at her.*) But
it's so ordinary . . . I came back . . . (*as he lights his cigarette*)
. . . expecting . . . ha (*laughing hysterically*) . . . I don't
know . . . and here I find you, smoking a cigarette . . .
you might have been tidying the room for the night. It's
so . . . ordinary. . . . (*After a pause, with a cry.*) Why don't
you *say* something!

DAN: I thought you were goin' to stay the night at
that feller's.

OLIVIA: I was.

DAN: What d'you come back for?

OLIVIA (*the words pouring out*): To find you out. You've
kept me guessing for a fortnight. Guessing hard. I very
nearly knew, all the time. But not quite. And now I do
know.

DAN: Why was you so keen on finding me out?

OLIVIA (*vehemently, coming to the table*): In the same way
any sane, decent-minded human would want – would
want to have you arrested for the monster you are!

DAN (*quietly*): What d'you come back for?

OLIVIA: I . . . I've told you. . . .

He smiles at her slowly and shakes his head. She sits at the table and closes her eyes.

I got as far as the edge of the wood. I could see the lights in the village . . . I came back.

She buries her head in her arms. DAN *rises, looks at her a moment regretfully, puts away his cigarette, and stands with both hands over the invalid chair.*

DAN (*casually*): She didn't keep any money anywhere else, did she?

OLIVIA: I've read a lot about evil——

DAN realises his hands are wet with paraffin and wipes them on his trousers.

DAN: Clumsy. . . .

OLIVIA: I never expected to come across it in real life.

DAN (*lightly*): You didn't ought to read so much. I never got through a book yet. . . . But I'll read you all right. . . . (*Crossing to her, leaning over the table, and smiling at her intently.*) You haven't had a drop of drink, and yet you feel as if you had. You never knew there was such a secret part inside of you. All that book-learnin' and moral-me-eye here and social-me-eye there – you took that off on the edge of the wood same as if it was an overcoat . . . and you left it there!

OLIVIA: I hate you. I . . . hate you!

DAN (*urgently*): And same as anybody out for the first time without their overcoat, you feel as light as air! Same as I feel, sometimes – only I never had no overcoat—— (*Excited.*) Why -- this is my big chance! You're the one I can tell about meself! Oh, I'm sick o' hearin' how clever everybody else is – I want to tell 'em how clever *I* am for a change! . . . Money I'm going to have, and people doin' what they're told, and *me* tellin' them to do it! There was a 'oman at the Tallboys, wasn't there? She wouldn't

be told, would she? She thought she was up 'gainst a
soft fellow in a uniform, didn't she? She never knew it
was *me* she was dealin' with – (*striking his chest in a paroxysm
of elation*) – *Me!* And this old girl treatin' me like a son
'cause I made her think she was a chronic invalid – ha!
She's been more use to me tonight (*tapping the notes in his
jacket pocket, smartly*) than she has to any other body all her
life. Stupid, that's what people are . . . stupid. If those
two hadn't been stupid they might be breathin' now;
you're not stupid; that's why I'm talkin' to you. (*With
exaggerated self-possession.*) You said just now murder's
ordinary. . . . Well it isn't ordinary at all, see? And I'm
not an ordinary chap. There's one big difference 'tween
me and other fellows that try this game. I'll *never be found
out.* 'Cause I don't care a—— (*snapping his fingers, grandly.*)
The world's goin' to hear from me. That's me. (*Chuckling.*)
You wait. . . . (*After a pause.*) But you can't wait, can
you?

OLIVIA: What do you mean?

DAN: Well, when I say I'll never be found out, what I
mean is, no living soul will be able to tell any other living
soul about me. (*Beginning to roll up a sleeve, nonchalantly.*)
Can you think of anybody . . . who can go tomorrow . . .
and tell the police the fire at Forest Corner . . . wasn't an
accident at all?

OLIVIA: I – I can.

DAN: Oh no, you can't.

OLIVIA: Why can't I?

DAN: Well, I'm up against a very serious problem, I
am. But the answer to it is as simple as pie, to a fellow like
me, simple as pie. . . . (*Rolling up the other sleeve a little way.*)
She isn't going to be the only one . . . found tomorrow
. . . in the fire at Forest Corner. . . . (*After a pause.*) Aren't

you frightened? You ought to be! (*Smiling.*) Don't you think I'll do it?

OLIVIA: I know you will. I just can't realise it.

DAN: You know, when I told you all that about meself just now, I'd made up my mind then about you. (*Moving slowly after her, round the table, as she steps back towards the window.*) That's what I am, see? I make up me mind to do a thing, and I do it.... You remember that first day when I come in here? I said to meself then, There's a girl that's got her wits about her; she knows a thing or two; different from the others. I was right, wasn't I? You—— (*Stopping abruptly, and looking round the room.*) What's that light in here?

OLIVIA: What light?

DAN: There's somebody in this room's holdin' a flash-light.

OLIVIA: It can't be in this room.... It must be a light in the wood.

DAN: It can't be.

    A flashlight crosses the window-curtain. OLIVIA *turns and stares at it.*

OLIVIA: Somebody's watching the bungalow....

    He looks at her, as if he did not understand.

DAN (*fiercely*): Nobody's watching! ...

    He runs to the window. She backs into the corner of the room.

I'm the one that watches! They've got no call to watch me! I'll go out and tell them that, an' all! (*Opening the curtains in a frenzy.*) I'm the one that watches!

    The light crosses the window again. He stares, then claps his hands over his eyes. Backing to the sofa.

Behind them trees. (*Clutching the invalid chair.*) Hundreds back of each tree.... Thousands of eyes. The whole damn world's on my track! . . . (*Sitting on the edge of the sofa, and listening.*) What's that? . . . Like a big wall fallin' over into the sea. . . . (*Closing his hands over his ears convulsively.*)

OLIVIA (*coming down to him*): They mustn't come in. . . .

DAN (*turning to her*): Yes, but . . . (*Staring.*) You're lookin' at me as if you never seen *me* before. . . .

OLIVIA: I never have. Nobody has. You've stopped acting at last. You're real. Frightened. Like a child. (*Putting her arm about his shoulders.*) They mustn't come in. . . .

DAN: But everything's slippin' away. From underneath our feet. . . . Can't you feel it? Starting slow . . . and then hundreds of miles an hour. . . . I'm goin' backwards! . . . And there's a wind in my ears, terrible blowin' wind. . . . Everything's going past me like the telegraph-poles. . . . All the things I've never seen . . . faster and faster . . . backwards – back to the day I was born. (*Shrieking.*) I can see it coming . . . the day I was born! . . . (*Turning to her, simply.*) I'm goin' to die. (*A pause. A knock at the front door.*) It's getting cold.

> *Another knock; louder. She presses his head to her.*

OLIVIA: It's all right. You won't die. I'll tell them I *made* you do it. I'll tell lies – I'll tell——

> *A third and louder knock at the front door. She realises that she must answer, goes into the hall, opens the front door, and comes back, hiding* DAN *from view.*

BELSIZE (*in the hall*): Good evening. . . . Sorry to pop back like this. . . .

> *He comes into the room, followed by* DORA *and* MRS TERENCE, *both terrified. Looking round.*

Everything looks all right here.

MRS TERENCE: I tell you we *did* 'ear her! Plain as plain! And we'd gone near a quarter of a mile——

DORA: Plain as plain——

MRS TERENCE: Made my blood run cold. 'Danny!' she screamed, 'Danny, where are you?' she said. She wanted 'im back, she did, to save 'er——

DORA: Because she was bein' murdered. I know it! I'd never a' run like that if I 'adn't 'eard——

BELSIZE: We'll soon find out who's right. . . . Now then—— (*As* OLIVIA *steps aside behind the sofa.*) Hello, Dan!

DAN (*quietly, rising and standing by the fireplace*): Hello.

BELSIZE (*standing behind the invalid chair*): Second time today, eh? . . .

DAN: That's right.

BELSIZE: How's the old lady?

DAN (*after a pause*): Not so bad, thanks, inspector! Gone to bed and says she didn't want to be disturbed——

BELSIZE: Smell of paraffin. . . .

DAN (*with a last desperate attempt at bluster*): You know what she's like, inspector, a bit nervy these days—— (*As* BELSIZE *goes to the bedroom and flashes a light into it.*) I'd no sooner got round the corner she screamed for me – 'Danny, Danny, Danny!' she was screaming – Danny she calls me, a pet name for Dan, that is——

> BELSIZE *goes into the sun-room.*

(*Rambling on mechanically.*) I told her so then. I said 'It's dangerous, that's what it is, havin' so much paraffin in the house.' That paraffin – she shouldn't ha' had so much paraffin in the house——

> *His voice trails away. Silence.* BELSIZE *comes back, his face intent, one hand in a coat pocket. A pause.*

BELSIZE (*to* OLIVIA): What are you doing here?

OLIVIA: I'm concerned in——

DAN (*loudly, decisively, silencing her*): It's all right. (*Cross-*

ing to BELSIZE *and swaggering desperately, in front of the women.*) I'm the fellow. Anything I'm concerned in, I run all by myself. If there's going to be any putting me on a public platform to answer any questions, I'm going to do it by myself . . . (*looking at* OLIVIA) . . . or not at all. I'll manage meself all right——

BELSIZE: I get you. Like a bit of limelight, eh?

DAN (*smiling*): Well . . .

BELSIZE (*as if humouring him*): Let's have a look at your hands, old boy, will you?

> *With an amused look at* OLIVIA, DAN *holds out his hands. Without warning,* BELSIZE *claps a pair of handcuffs over his wrists.* DAN *stares at them a moment, then sits on the sofa, and starts to pull at them furiously over his knee. He beats at them wildly, moaning and crying like an animal. He subsides gradually, looks at the others and rises.*

DAN (*muttering, holding his knee*): Hurt meself. . . .

BELSIZE: That's better. . . . Better come along quietly. . . .

> *He goes up towards the hall.* DAN *follows him, and takes his hat from the occasional table. As he puts it on he catches sight of his face in the mirror.*

BELSIZE (*to the others, crisply, during this*): I've a couple of men outside. I'll send 'em in. See that nothing's disturbed. . . . Coming, old chap?

DORA: What's 'e doin'?

MRS TERENCE: He's lookin' at himself in the glass. . . .

> *A pause.*

DAN (*speaking to the mirror*): This is the real thing, old boy. Actin'. . . . That's what she said, wasn't it? She was right, you know . . . I've been playing up to you, haven't I? I showed you a trick or two, didn't I? . . . But this is the real thing. (*Swaying.*) Got a cigarette? . . . (*Seeing* OLIVIA.) You're not goin' to believe what she said? About helpin' me?

BELSIZE (*humouring him*): No. (*Putting a cigarette between* DAN's *lips and lighting it.*) Plenty of women get a bit hysterical about a lad in your position. You'll find 'em queueing up all right when the time comes. Proposals of marriage by the score.

DAN (*pleased*): Will they?

BELSIZE: Come along——

    DAN *turns to follow him.* DORA *is in the way.*

DAN: Oh yes . . . I forgot about you. . . . (*Smiling, with a curious detached sadness.*) Poor little fellow. Poor little chap. . . . (*Looking round.*) You know, I'd like somethin' now I never wanted before. A long walk, all by meself. And just when I can't have it. (*Laughing.*) That's contrary, isn't it?

BELSIZE (*sternly*): Coming?

DAN (*looking at* OLIVIA): Just comin'.

    He goes to OLIVIA, *takes out his cigarette, puts his manacled arms round her, and kisses her suddenly and violently on the mouth. He releases her with an air of bravado, puts back his cigarette, and looks at her.*

DAN: Well, I'm goin' to be hanged in the end. . . . But they'll get their money's worth at the trial. You wait!

    He smiles, and raises his hand to his hat-brim with the old familiar jaunty gesture of farewell. He walks past BELSIZE *and out through the front door.* BELSIZE *follows him. The bang of the front door.* OLIVIA *falls to the sofa. The sound of* DORA'S *sobbing.*

CURTAIN